12
KEY STEPS TO BUILD
HIGH CONFIDENCE

THE MASTER KEY TO YOUR POWER

GITI CARAVAN

BALBOA.
PRESS

A DIVISION OF HAY HOUSE

Balboa Press books may be ordered through booksellers or by contacting:

Balboa Press
A Division of Hay House
1663 Liberty Drive
Bloomington, IN 47403
www.balboapress.com
1 (877) 407-4847

Because of the dynamic nature of the Internet, any web addresses or links contained in this book may have changed since publication and may no longer be valid. The views expressed in this work are solely those of the author and do not necessarily reflect the views of the publisher, and the publisher hereby disclaims any responsibility for them.

The author of this book does not dispense medical advice or prescribe the use of any technique as a form of treatment for physical, emotional, or medical problems without the advice of a physician, either directly or indirectly. The intent of the author is only to offer information of a general nature to help you in your quest for emotional and spiritual well-being. In the event you use any of the information in this book for yourself, which is your constitutional right, the author and the publisher assume no responsibility for your actions.

Any people depicted in stock imagery provided by Getty Images are models, and such images are being used for illustrative purposes only. Certain stock imagery © Getty Images.

Print information available on the last page.

ISBN: 978-1-9822-2112-6 (sc)
ISBN: 978-1-9822-2111-9 (hc)
ISBN: 978-1-9822-2114-0 (e)

Library of Congress Control Number: 2019901123

Balboa Press rev. date: 09/04/2019

PRAISE FOR

12 KEY STEPS TO BUILD HIGH CONFIDENCE
– THE MASTER KEY TO YOUR POWER

"To be successful, you must have confidence. Follow Giti Caravan's advice to increase your self-confidence and step more boldly through life."

Bob Proctor

Great Master Teacher of success and love of attraction – As featured in the Movie "The Secret"

CONTENTS

SECTION THREE
The 12 Positive Habits Of Mind That Build Confidence

SECTION FOUR
Effect of Confidence on Health and Wealth

FOREWORD

I am deeply grateful Giti decided to write this very important book on the subject of confidence. By the time you complete this book, you will also feel a wonderful sense of appreciation as her only desire is to help you experience a more fulfilling life.

In the first chapter you will discover that you will be inspired to take your life from where you are to where you want to be, and this book is the perfect solution to accomplish just that.

Confidence is one of the most important aspects of success. If you have a healthy sense of confidence, you can almost write your own ticket to success. Without confidence, you will struggle all the days of your life.

Many years ago, I had extremely low confidence, although that is not the case today. As a child, I was raised in a dysfunctional and abusive home. Please understand that I am not blaming my parents, as I believe, they simply did the best they could with what they knew. However, as a result of being raised in a dysfunctional environment, I was extremely insecure and had very low confidence. It wasn't until I began the journey of self-improvement that everything changed.

I was close to 20 years of age when I made a decision to change my life by changing me. At the time of writing this Foreword, I have been studying success for 40 years and my life has changed in every wonderful way. I am thankful this world is blessed with many teachers, authors, experts who teach the wisdom of taking control of your life. You should, likewise, feel blessed, that Giti, who has 30 years of experience as a psychotherapist with clinical and educational psychology background, is sharing this important and valuable material with you.

Let's think of the word "confidence" as an emotion that has different levels of intensity. Low level of confidence would appear as insecurity, a high level of confidence would be portrayed as a person who is self-assured. Confidence is not boastful or arrogant. In fact, a true confident person is one who has a quiet calm about them.

As you go through this book take an honest look at yourself. Giti shares a number of ways that people rob themselves of confidence. It is in the understanding that you will know yourself and be able to make some positive change.

You will discover that (as the great Master Teacher Bob Proctor taught me many years ago) ... "no amount of reading will bring you anything – it isn't until you seek to have the understanding and apply the wisdom of success that your life will change". You will be pleased to discover that Giti gives you the wisdom in order to have the understanding AND she also shares suggestions for how to apply these wise thoughts into your life. Follow through with her recommendations and watch your life change in only wonderful and glorious ways.

Peggy McColl,
New York Times Best Selling Author

PREFACE

The fact that you are reading these pages and initiating this step at this particular time in your life's journey is not random. Rather, consider this as a sign that your desire to understand yourself and your passion have come together to direct you to make profound changes in your life. The knowledge you will gain from this book will aid you in building the confidence required to grow and succeed in your life.

The countless examples, anecdotes, insights, and pieces of advice provided in this book are the result of my thousands of encounters with clients of all walks of life throughout my 30-year career in counselling, psychology, and psychotherapy.

This book is intended for those who have identified a need for, and are ready to make a commitment to, building higher confidence. It contains proven processes, procedures, and steps to be followed to achieve your desired outcomes and advance from not trusting yourself to believing and having confidence in yourself.

Please read this book to the end – the concepts are explained in an easy-to-follow manner and outline a system that will help you, regardless of the stage of life in which you find yourself. Whether you want to start building confidence in your life, or simply want to take your confidence to the next level, this book will be a valuable resource. The material will give you powerful yet simple formulas to guide you step-by-step towards building high confidence with pride and satisfaction.

This book will prepare you for growth and, when combined with readiness to embrace the possibilities, will constitute a great recipe for confidence. This recipe is nothing more than readiness to embrace opportunities and well-timed moments coming together.

ACKNOWLEDGMENTS

I would like to humbly and deeply acknowledge and appreciate my late mother who always believed in me, inspired me, filled my life with positive energy, and taught me to put highest values in learning. She instilled in me the "I can do it" belief. I would like to honour and appreciate my late father from the bottom of my heart, for he taught me to contribute generously to others and see goodness in everyone.

In addition, I would like to extend my affectionate gratitude to my husband, my soulmate, who has always supported me in my journey and motivated me to learn and grow. I would like to extend a big bouquet of gratefulness to the bundles of joy in my life, my children, Rose, Shawn, and Sara, who have been the most significant sources of revelation in my life.

Thank you, Rose! You were born focused and curious. Your burning desire to learn, and your inquisitive search to know more about everything never ceases to amaze me. You have given me an eternal drive to be ambitious and become a life-long learner.

Thank you, Shawn! You were born eager to learn; have always had the perseverance and determination to perceive life as a school, and to learn from everything and every experience. You inspire me to have the conviction to be the leader of my own life with purpose.

And thank you, Sara! You are unreal; you leap to the next phase of learning always. You have been visionary, sharp, spontaneous, and a spark of light in my life.

You all have given me the drive to strive and soar towards growth, every day.

INTRODUCTION

"As soon as you trust yourself, you will know how to live."

Johann Wolfgang von Goethe

As a psychotherapist, counsellor, business consultant, trainer of hypnotherapy and neuro-linguistic programming, and leadership coach, I frequently come across people who struggle to achieve something but they just don't seem to get the results they want. After spending many years trying to understand why this happens, I realized that there is a common theme; most of these individuals do not get the intended results because they do not have the right recipe for success.

If we think of every area of life as a meal, then a main difference between an incredible meal and one that does not have the desired taste is the recipe. Indeed, a recipe provides the quantities of all ingredients, order of operation, and cooking time that make the meal a success. However, if you bake a cake that does not taste as expected, it might be because the recipe was not properly followed. When I listen to people's stories, there is often a gap between the place they are and the place they want to be. This gap is caused by missing a key ingredient; doing things in the wrong order, or misallocating the amount of time they put into achieving their goals. Often, they spend too much time on minor things and too little time on major things.

In this book, I will show you the right recipe for going from living doubtfully to living purposefully and confidently. Use this book and you will know what to do to achieve the high level of confidence you are seeking.

As mentioned in the Preface, the fact that you happened to stumble upon this book is not random. You must have had a desire to take your life to the next level, and you came to the right place. When you get a chance, take a quick look at your life and make an inventory list of your actions. This can help you realize whether you have taken all the actions you had planned to take in order to achieve your goals and, if not, what the reasons might be. In this book, I will review some of the potential reasons behind your lack of progress towards your goals and outline how to take those actions.

Confidence is the desire and ability to learn. If you are too confident, you feel you know it all and do not have the desire to learn and grow; therefore, you become stale and use a mask of arrogance to cover your insecurities. If you have low confidence, you might have the desire to learn but do not think of yourself as a capable learner; therefore, you get stuck in fear and show insecurity. In both cases, you will not learn or grow. In order to grow, you must have the right amount of confidence, which is the desire to learn and the ability to see yourself as capable of learning.

The focus of this book is not so much on "why you lack confidence", but rather on "how to build high confidence". You may lack confidence because of your upbringing or because a very well-intended parent suppressed your confidence. Or perhaps a dear family member, friend, or acquaintance damaged your confidence. Whatever the reason, view this book as your map or recipe to build confidence. Any time you feel lost, come back to it to find your way out.

"Self-confidence is the first requisite to great undertakings."
Samuel Johnson

SECTION ONE
THE IMPORTANCE OF CONFIDENCE

Chapter One:
What Is Confidence?

"I was always looking outside myself for strength and confidence but it comes from within. It is there all the time."

Anna Freud

You can have faith either in your strengths or in your limitations. When you have faith in your limitations, you feel despair, but when you have faith in your abilities, you become inspired.

Confidence comes from **what you think about your abilities**. In other words, confidence is a self-perception that you have in the core of your being. What you think about yourself will show in your actions. Having power comes from being at harmony with yourself, *knowing yourself*, and being connected with your inner strength. You can then be free from your limitations and become an exceptional person who is reliant on own strengths. When the creative side of you rises, you become curious about your abilities, are not afraid to act, and are not afraid to move towards achieving your vision.

Being at peace with yourself allows you to capitalize on your strengths, which then builds confidence. Having a positive attitude about your abilities and transforming those abilities into actions is a source of wealth and power. When you harness your power, you master your potential and can reach what you desire. You are then confident and ready to do whatever it takes to reach your goal. When you do things that once seemed impossible and you thought were beyond your abilities, you gain strength, courage, and confidence. You begin to trust that you are able to do anything. Confidence comes from the way you think about your abilities, and the way that you think about your abilities affects your performance. It's a magic circle; if you think you can do it, then you take action and do it, and gain more confidence along the way. The inner power that you gain by doing the hardest thing is the seed of confidence that will foster confidence into your future.

Confidence is like your appearance, but it is one of the qualities from your inner wardrobe. You cannot wear all of your wardrobe at once, but how you wear different pieces shows your taste, creativity, and resourcefulness. You have resources in your inner wardrobe that you mix and match to show who you are. To make the best of your resources, you pick the ones that suit you the most, according to the situation you face. The greater your confidence, the more resourceful you become in using the resources you have. You can fulfill your highest potential by being more resourceful and creative, which results in making complicated situations simpler.

If you want to be confident, you *must* learn to think confidently. Confidence is the strong belief that you have about yourself. In other words, confidence is how you see yourself in your mind. These beliefs will start to show in your actions; you start to perform and act confidently.

Building confidence is a journey, not a destination. To become more confident, you must be passionate in your pursuit of a more significant future. Confidence can also be viewed as a chain of habitual actions. First you make a wish, then you fulfill your wish by achieving your goal, and, finally, take pride in what you have achieved.

Confidence is a set of mental skills that you can build. Self-confidence is something that you learn to develop, and one that will continue to develop as long as you practice your skills. Being confident depends on a combination of good physical health, emotional health, and social health. The challenges of life — be they physical, mental, or social — generally deflate self-confidence. For example, any mental health disorder or emotional trauma can damage self-confidence, just as any physical illness or challenge may also put a dent in your confidence. In contrast, recovery from those illnesses or overcoming those challenges helps to build confidence.

Furthermore, social crises such as gossip, backstabbing, and humiliation can substantially reduce your confidence. Responding to and rebounding from these challenges is what strengthens confidence.

Focus on your abilities. Self-confidence comes from believing in yourself and having the skills to back up those beliefs with actions. The fact that you have talents and have experienced success will motivate you to do more. As the ancient proverb says, "nothing succeeds like success". You cannot be good at everything and cannot be confident all the time because you are not a machine; only a mechanical device can be perfect all the time. However, being able to think positively makes the difference between a successful person and an unsuccessful one. While both might fall, only the successful person bounces back quickly as the unsuccessful stays down.

Faith in your abilities is confidence. Confidence is peace of mind, the master key where all power lies. Confidence opens the door to health, joy, and wisdom. Confidence is faith in yourself and belief in your unseen potential. Self-confidence is being ready for life's opportunities as they present themselves. Having some faith in yourself and your abilities — even those you have not yet seen — will give you the courage you need to take action in your life.

Your power lies within you. The only way you can unleash your power is to be confident. Now that we defined confidence, let's talk about the importance of building confidence.

Chapter Two: Why is it Important to Build Self-confidence?

"When you have confidence, you can have a lot of fun. And when you have fun, you can do amazing things."

Joe Namath

Everyone knows that self-confidence is important. However, as a therapist, I have witnessed that confidence is truly essential. Having high confidence affects your levels of happiness, health, and well-being. Being confident is empowering because you have power over your own life. You have the strength to know that you have the resources to deal with whatever comes your way. Self-confidence can change your whole life for the better because you become the power in your own world. A lack of confidence, on the other hand, takes the joy out of life. To put simply, self-confidence and happiness are firmly connected and correlated.

Confidence is contagious. When you are confident and at peace with yourself, you have more harmony with others and your own life. Confidence is a positive outlook towards yourself, and this can impact and inspire others.

Confidence breeds ambition. When you build high confidence, you are more realistic in the way you see yourself as being capable, without needing the approval of others. You become a lofty dreamer and have the courage to pursue your dreams like they are your life's mission. You will follow your dreams, which will lead to success.

When you are confident, you believe that you are capable of being happy regardless of your achievements.

No persons are required to determine if you are capable or not, just as no conditions are required to determine if you are capable or not. As a confident person, you have a strong sense of self and self-trust. You know what you like and what you don't, yet at the same time you are open-minded. You have most likely built a strong sense of self by having a wide variety of experiences. Confidence and success are contagious and inter-connected. Having confidence brings success, and success brings more success as you become more confident.

When you don't have confidence, you think you can't do a good job and, guess what, you won't. It's not your 'ability', it's your 'availability' that makes the difference. When you are confident and think confidently, you are more available for opportunities. Because you are available to take the challenge and meet the opportunity, success can happen. As so succinctly put by Roman philosopher Seneca,

> *"Luck is what happens when preparation meets opportunity*

After briefly talking about the importance of confidence, let's consider how low confidence can be harmful.

Chapter Three: Harms of Lacking Confidence

"It's not the lack of ability or opportunity that holds you back; it is only a lack of confidence in yourself."
Richard Monckton Milnes

A lack of confidence is akin to welcoming fear. When there is room in you for fear, it gradually becomes the chief commander of your life. If you let fear get the best of you, then your life becomes a series of unfortunate events. Fear creates its own energy as well as a host of missed opportunities.

Lack of self-confidence can create depression. Confidence stems from realizing that you are more significant than your doubts and worries. Lack of confidence is the hole that drains the joy from your life and relationships (personal, professional, and social). Fear is the result of a lack of faith in yourself, which can project to the outside world as self-doubt. Lack of confidence is the result of not knowing what you can do.

When you don't take the risk of taking action, you are not aware of your abilities. Your experience teaches you and at the same time reveals who you are. In fact, people differ in how they respond to failure. If you fall on the way to your destination and get up again, you learn by experience. This is the root of practical knowledge that shapes your expertise. Lack of expertise is the result of a lack of doing something new or a lack of experience.

When you lack confidence in yourself, you cannot have confidence in anybody else. This lack of confidence might also result in being critical and impulsive in your relationships.

Confidence and happiness are intercorrelated; when you are more confident, you are happy for no apparent reason. Lack of confidence is also related to depression. We all want a life that fills us with ease, peace, and happiness. However, along the way we create many problems that can make us either stronger and happier if we learn to become resilient, or miserable and depressed if we give in.

Perhaps the biggest harm of low confidence is not just the loss of opportunities but a failure to strive to be more than what you are. Both confidence and fear (which will be discussed later) are contagious. Lack of confidence makes you blind towards all of the opportunities that are available to you, and even prevents you from enjoying what you have already done, because you can't give yourself credit. Lack of confidence causes procrastination and holds you back from achieving your greatest potential.

As an individual, you might be influenced both positively and negatively by others. If you lack self-confidence, you might be more susceptible to the negative suggestions of others. You basically hear what is in harmony with your way of thinking and what reinforces the way that you focus on your weaknesses. Hence, your weaknesses grow. Remember that *your energy flows wherever your focus goes.*

One of the worst things that can happen with lack of confidence is that you stay stuck in one place and don't do anything to change your situation. You can only move forward if you are open to new ways of thinking. Unfortunately, negative emotions such as anger, hatred, jealousy, and shame are generally more potent than positive emotions. When you are controlled by your negative emotions, you lose confidence. Lack of confidence can make you inactive, passive, and stuck.

An insecure and overly sensitive character comes from a profound sense of self-doubt, and a deep feeling of uncertainty about your fundamental self and your place in the world. Insecurity is the result of chronic feelings of inadequacy, which stem from low self- perception and anxiety about your relationships with people.

After talking about how harmful a lack of confidence can be, we are ready to discuss how negative habits of thinking must be replaced with positive ones in order to build confidence.

THE 12 HABITS OF MIND THAT ROB YOU OF CONFIDENCE

INTRODUCTION

You look at the world through the same lens you use to look at yourself. Inadequacies in abilities come from a lack of confidence in your way of thinking. Lack of confidence is like living with handcuffs, which is the severest kind of restraint because the person who put the handcuffs on you *is yourself.* The ultimate restraint is what people put on themselves. The worst thing person believes that other people, situations, and things control their lives, this becomes so fully fixed in their thinking that they are offended even by logical arguments that prove otherwise. You cannot change your life unless you change your way of thinking.

To think and feel that your life is dominated by another individual, group, or society forces a condition of mental drudgery that makes you a fugitive of your own making. When you try so hard to fit in, like a chameleon who changes its color to fit into its environment, you become drained and exhausted. You may feel hopeless that you will never be the same color as others. When you try so hard to be similar to the majority, you lose the courage to be yourself. This does not make you a coward, but it makes you a conformist.

Many people think the only thing that they need in order to change their lives is willpower. This is not even close to being true. As Shakespeare said,

"We know what we are, but not what we may be".

Therefore, you must shift the way of your thinking in order to change your life. A negative way of thinking causes people to be their own number one enemy. For a negative thinker, as much as they try to move towards their goals, they actually move further away from their goals. Because they have accepted a false belief as fact, it becomes their natural way of behaving. All of their abilities, good intentions, efforts, and willpower are impotent against the powerful false belief they have accepted as truth. As William James, the famous philosopher and psychologist said,

> *"The greatest discovery of our age has been that we, by changing the inner aspects of our thinking, can change the outer aspects of our lives."*

You are about to take a journey that will repay you for the rest of your life. You are going to discover to avoid the cracks that are the restraints that have been holding you back. These are ways of thinking that rob you of confidence and make your life a big drama. The ensuing chapters describe the 12 ways of thinking that rob you of confidence and create a limited life.

Chapter One: Being Fearful

"F-E-A-R has two meanings: 'Forget Everything And Run' or 'Face Everything And Rise'. The choice is yours."

Zig Ziglar

F-E-A-R can also be considered an acronym for False Evidence Assumed Reality, because fear is nothing but an illusion. Fear brings doubt and breaks you to pieces and, therefore, robs you of confidence. If you run from your fear, you will develop anxiety and depression; if you face your fear, you will build strength. In fact, one of the primary reasons for experiencing anxiety is seeing what might go wrong in a given situation rather than seeing what great things could come out of the situation. Fear causes you to doubt your ability to handle a situation and makes you a miserable fortune teller. If you are confident, however, you think you can handle the situation properly and hence won't feel anxious.

Running away from your fears sabotages your social relationships, hinders your career achievements, and even adversely affects your mood. When you are confident, you know your own values, and thus can face your fears and feel less discouraged upon being rejected. In reality, no one can reject you except you, because you deny yourself your values. Rejection is only real when you accept it as rejection; otherwise rejection is just feedback from others. *To face your fear of rejection, you must know that rejection is for your protection.* In other words, you were protected from further harm by being rejected, be it *in the form of a rejection letter, relationship rejection, or personal rejection.*

For strong people, hearing 'NO' is not devastating because for them it can be considered an acronym for Next Opportunity. What makes many people feel down when they are denied or told NO is their own lack of confidence in their abilities and not the rejection itself.

The best way to overcome fear is to face it head on. If you gather up courage and do something that scares you, then that experience becomes something that can help you conquer your other fears. You build yourself up every day and gain confidence from every experience. So, get out of your comfort zone and face your fears! You can choose to just live, or use your courage and feel alive. Every time you confront your fear, you show a sign of courage and tap into your power. Sometimes you must tell yourself to "hang in there" — you are closer to success than you might think. If you follow this advice, you will fill your bucket slowly with every drop, and before you know it, you realize that your bucket is full. As Dale Carnegie said,

> *"Face the thing that seems overwhelming, and you will be surprised how your fear melts away".*

As much as fear drains the joy and energy out of your life, conquering fears is essential in building confidence.

> *"If you want to take control of your life you have to stop hating and fearing, then you become liberated and will have control over your life."*
>
> Michael Jordan

Now that we talked about fear, let's talk about another negative habit that can be a reason for lack of confidence for some people.

Chapter Two: Being a Perfectionist

"To achieve the greatest success, you have to embrace the prospect of failure."

Pauline Estrem

In my practice, I have noticed many people value the perfectionist personality, mainly because, to them, perfectionism equals achievement. Some of these individuals have a phobia of making mistakes, while others think that being a perfectionist is an achievement in itself or that it at least helps them appear to be high achievers. The truth is that those striving for perfection can be very different from those striving for excellence.

A perfectionist is displeased by any achievement that is less than 100%. Perfectionists might easily give up if they encounter obstacles because they live far from reality. Perfectionism indeed drives people to be idealists who are also unrealistic, because they attempt to achieve an unattainable ideal. The problem with perfectionists is that their evaluation system is outside of them and they want to impress others. In other words, their evaluation system is dependent on the praise of others. Perfectionists think they must reach self-perfection to reach self-acceptance.

As discussed earlier, a person who needs to impress others to feel good about themselves is lacking in confidence. In contrast, a person who has a drive for excellence only strives to do their best. They measure themselves by their effort, not by the results or the measure of others. A person who works towards excellence enjoys his/her success rather than only seeking perfection.

A perfectionist is someone who only sees the glass as half empty; only sees what is missing or what part is not "perfect", and therefore cannot be satisfied and happy. Because all that matters is winning, perfectionists do not place much value in the effort itself. All of the boxes must be check-marked or nothing is acceptable. However, because we live in a world where *nothing is perfect*, the perfectionist is, in effect, looking for something that doesn't exist.

To attain some satisfaction, a perfectionist's high standards are therefore applied towards small things. Although perfectionism can sometimes motivate the perfectionist, they can easily get disappointed and fall into depression, if they cannot reach their goals. This is largely because their happiness is highly dependent on their performance and what they have to show for it at the end.

Perhaps the biggest problem with perfectionists is that they are afraid of starting new tasks because they must know all of the details ahead of time. Because all that matters is "perfect" results, they cannot take any risks of walking into something new if they don't know if they can finish it perfectly. Perfectionists get stuck as they wait for the perfect opportunity to present itself. Because they must know everything in advance, they are afraid of surprises and want to have guaranteed results without serious challenges or unknowns. However, *when there are no challenges there are no changes.*

Perfectionists are afraid to fail; therefore, safety becomes the most important element to hold on to. But, more often than not, they end up being sorry if they remain attached only to safety. The greatest successes come with the biggest failures. Just consider the case of Thomas Edison. His most memorable invention was the light bulb, which purportedly took 1,000 tries before he developed a successful prototype.

> *"How did it feel to fail 1,000 times?"*, a reporter asked.

"I didn't fail 1,000 times", Edison responded. *"The light bulb was an invention with 1,000 steps".*

The perfectionist has high expectations for themselves and others, so much so that they feel burdened by the sheer number of expectations. The perfectionist feels that they sacrifice many of their needs for others, work more than others, but are not appreciated enough. Consequently, they don't feel good about themselves. Even the sweetest victory does not mean much to them, and they don't appreciate that success. Perfectionists are often overwhelmed by tasks, yet are unable to ask for help because no one can do anything as well as they can. They have many rules for themselves and others. At the same time, they don't feel good enough because they place unrealistic expectations on themselves and others.

People who are confident become more capable and take on the role of movers and shakers. The confident are more realistic and not idealistic; they know they can achieve what they want to, if they work hard. At the same time, they are not wishful thinkers; they know it takes hard work and recognize that they may not always succeed in completing the task. Those who have been in the trenches, survived battles, and come home alive, have irreplaceable experience and perseverance.

Therefore, the recipe I recommend for perfectionists is to understand that you cannot do everything yourself and be good at everything. Accept that fact and free yourself. We are put on Earth and given the freedom to choose. We as humans are figuring it all out as we go. A person who needs to know everything beforehand is claiming they are bigger than the universe. Try to learn as you go. If you do not take risks and make mistakes, you will never learn. Success comes from failure. When you make a mistake, the mistake itself becomes an experience and if you learn a lesson from the experience, then the next time you will make better choices. Therefore, ironically, success can come from making mistakes, if you view them as learning opportunities which would lead to making better choices. Having courage to take action builds more confidence, and the best thing a perfectionist can do is to take action no matter how small the action and no matter what the results are. Even if you don't get the results you expected, you will gain the experience and either way you are building your confidence.

Now let's discuss another habit of thinking that you have to avoid to be able to become more confident.

Chapter Three: Being Anxious

"Failure feelings - fear, anxiety, lack of self-confidence - do not spring from some heavenly oracle. They are not written in the stars. They are not holy gospel. Nor are they intimations of a set and decided fate which means that failure is decreed and decided. They originate from your own mind."

Maxwell Maltz

While confidence is a rebellious action against fear, anxiety is loyalty to a perceived threat. Confidence is defiance against fear, while anxiety is dependence on the fear. Confidence is a sort of contempt and a feeling of superiority in the face of anxiety, whereas anxiety is a sort of subordination to the imagined threat and a feeling of inferiority in life. Confidence is a resolution to allow hope to breathe in and to find determination by having faith and taking actions, which is the only way out of the imagined threat. You cannot escape fear, you must be brave and go through it. The road to confidence passes through the dark tunnel of anxieties.

Anxiety diminishes confidence. Life is about taking risks, starting from uncertainty, and leaving your comfort zone to reach the other side of the anxiety, which is where your dreams lie.

In the face of anxiety, you must have hope because this is the only thing you can hang on to when you don't have anything else. To be confident, you must act inside your *strength* zone and outside your *comfort* zone. Anxiety is the feeling that stems from looking to gain either confidence from others, the approval of others, or both.

When you have anxiety, you live in the circle of fight or flight. You invest your energy in negativity and focus on your doubts and total lack of faith in your abilities. Consequently, you force yourself to be peaceful, but the 'peace' that comes with 'force' is anxiety.

A normal human life will always have some dark days, and they will pass; but, if because of the imagined threat you go and hide in a cave, you will stay in the dark. The most certain way to end the dark is to take *action*, to allow the light in. It's not the storm that ruins everything, it's what you do after the storm and how you deal with its consequences that matter.

The hardest victory is the victory over yourself. When you allow your anxious feelings to linger, you will be terrorized solely by your own feelings. This is a recipe for troubles to arise, and a sure way out is for you to face what makes you anxious and rise above it. One way to achieve this is to only care about your dreams and not your dreads.

Anxiety arises from a longing to be the person you think others want you to be. It is what makes your plate overflow with expectations that you assume others have of you, and what makes you search for their approval. Anxious feelings can come from realizing that you are living by the expectations of others while you are in the midst of becoming who you want to be.

Remember, however, that a certain amount of anxiety can indicate you are at the beginning of living a conscious life; that is, you are not on autopilot. To recognize who you are, you need to know who you are trying to please and by whose expectations you are living. Being out of alignment with your true self can create anxiety. Conversely, trying to control other people's lives can cause anxiety as well. When you want others to be interested in you, you are anxious and have no confidence; when you become the person who you are interested in, you become confident and interesting.

As indicated above, a small amount of anxiety is not necessarily a bad thing. Rather, what matters is how you handle your anxious moments; that is what determines if your anxiety works for you or against you. You can become free from anxiety by having the audacity to accept the pain of others' disapproval and stay true to your authentic self, no matter how frightened you are. But have no doubt, at some point some people will criticize your choices, but you won't despair if you know how to refuel your courage to carry on. You cannot be consumed by what others think of you, you cannot continue to seek outside approval, and you cannot continue trying to impress others while at the same time staying confident. When you are nervous, then you are needy, particularly for the approval of others. Simply put, you cannot need anyone's approval and have confidence at the same time.

If you are in a constant state of social anxiety, deep down you are looking for love, attention, and the approval of others. Unfortunately, this road has never led anyone to happiness. When you are constantly looking for the love and approval of others, you continuously doubt yourself and live a life that lacks peace of mind. Similarly, when you find yourself in an eternal journey to impress others, you pay the price by becoming anxious and losing self-confidence.

If you keep doubting yourself and intensely search for validity that comes from the outside, your confidence will indeed be in the hands of others. Your strongest link then becomes your weakest link. If you look for peace of mind that comes from the approval of others, you will not find it. In fact, this lack of peace of mind can create more worry and anxiety. When you do not approve of yourself, you are needy, nervous, and riddled with doubt. Your wish for self-confidence will never come true until you learn to validate yourself. The quickest route to self-confidence is to possess an attitude of 'no fear'. To be confident, you have to be on the front lines of your own life, confront your anxieties, and rise above them.

Confidence will show itself when you **leave the safety of the comfort zone that holds you back.** If you want to permanently remain in your comfort zone, you will end up being sorry. One of the biggest secrets of becoming confident is operating in unfamiliar territory. Life is filled with unknowns and, when you doubt yourself, you get anxious and cannot step into the unknown. The good news is that, when you face your anxiety, you will conquer them. When people are anxious, in most cases it is because they suffer from low confidence and have lost trust in themselves. Life is constantly evolving. Life takes place in uncertainty, and you start from this place of uncertainty to reach certainty. Anything that you want to do in life requires you to have some degree of conviction and confidence in your abilities. Surrendering to anxiety eats up your confidence from within, like termites in wood; as a result, you can become hollow. If you find yourself in a place of anxiety, remember that it is a place that you must pass through, because staying there will paralyze you and you will become stuck.

Thus, if you operate with an anxious mind then you must test your thoughts to find out which of the false concepts you have accepted as your truth. Once you surrender yourself to one false concept, it becomes easy to surrender yourself to more false concepts. As a result, it becomes easy to act anxiously and with low confidence.

We will next talk about another habit of thinking that you must avoid in order to build more confidence.

Chapter Four: Controlling Behavior

"Lack of confidence is what makes you want to change somebody else's mind. When you're OK, you don't need to convince anyone else in order to empower yourself."

Jada Pinkett Smith

People who want to control others want everything to be perfect in their environment. They think they are in charge of everything and see themselves as actually being in charge of others. Because of this assumption, these people like to be really prepared in every way and they see others as incapable. They only want to do what they want to do, but at the same time they are afraid that other peoples' freedom might interfere with what they like to do. Therefore, controlling personalities are really terrified when they are not in control of what is going on, what others are doing, or what is going to happen in the future.

A controlling personality makes rules and instructions for people around them, in order for themselves to feel free. Others have to report to them and act based on the controlling person's instructions so that the controller would feel safe and calm. When you face controlling people and tell them they want to control others, they may actually like it; some may freely admit that they are indeed control-freaks because they are striving to be in control.

On the other hand, anything that makes a controlling person feel out of control makes them uncomfortable.

They want you to know how to do everything that makes them happy, but you must also share everything with them; if you don't, they feel out of control and become impulsive and over-reactive. A controlling individual is also very anxious and has a tendency to micromanage others, making everyone around them feel very stressed out. Ironically, they themselves are also stressed out because they want to police everyone and this can be exhausting. They force their rules on others and demand obedience from others but, in reality, the only thing that is out of their control is their own life.

The root of control is fear and anxiety. Controlling behavior brews anger and frustration because controlling people often feel things are out of their control. Unfortunately, they think it is their right to rule other people's lives, and if others don't give in to their control they become vindictive and claim the moral high ground to regain that control. They see themselves as ethical, while they are often far from it. They want to continue controlling others because it benefits them while making others' lives miserable. When someone is doing something, the controlling individual watches from the corner of their eye and feels an urge to give feedback, which is usually negative and critical, because they themselves are nervous and needy.

The only joy in the lives of controlling people is when they think they are proven right, are seen as the boss, or have the last word in an argument. They usually do not invite co-operation and never inspire others; all they do is tell others what to do. However, the lives of controlling people are a vicious cycle; they need to be in control to feel confident but their controlling behavior kills their confidence every day. Their need to be in control erodes their confidence and breeds more insecurity because they want to gain confidence by controlling the uncontrollable, which is everyone else.

People who have control issues suffer from a lack of confidence. They are very insecure; the way they learned to live their lives was to focus on controlling others and not themselves, so they eventually go out of control. They lose trust in themselves because they cannot control everyone. They think they know what other people think, need, want, and should do, but the only person they are oblivious to is themselves. Losing touch with themselves is what makes them less confident and more insecure. Their thinking is so distorted that they put their happiness in the hands of others. Their strongest link is their weakest link because they control others but the level of their happiness is controlled by others: *"If you behave the way I want you to, I will be better"*. Although they may momentarily feel a bit better when they get their way, overall they cannot be happy. The reason for their lack of happiness is that their direction in life is the exact opposite of becoming more confident. Confident people only demand from themselves, not anyone else.

Controlling people are filled with resentment, and manipulate other people's emotional lives to gain control of them. They do this sometimes by being angry and sometimes by being very nice. They fail to recognize that they will never be able to control someone's emotional response. Angry people do not have self-control because they want to control others. You lose power when you cannot recognize what you can and cannot change.

Just remind yourself that you did not come to this world to be a control fanatic. You were born to take care of yourself and to be in charge of your own life. When you are confident, you lead your own life and it is your mission to do so. Consider yourself part of the same energy as others, which means you are in harmony with the rest of the world. Just learn to interact, not for survival, but for joy and growth. What you sow is what you reap, so if you continue to try to control others, you feed your insecurity, lack of confidence, and, worst of all, anger and misery.

The following is another habit of thinking that you have to avoid to be able to become more confident.

Chapter Five: Being Doubtful

"To find yourself living with doubt might feel such a curse. There is a kind of worship in trying to search for truth, even before the first fight has been found."

Deepak Chopra

Living in constant doubt is the worst kind of living; it is like living under the spell of constant fear. When you are afraid of moving forward and are stuck in past mistakes, you are searching for truth through a lens of doubt. The lens of doubt is out of alignment with reality. Your truth cannot be proven, while doubts can be proven wrong. There is no need to prove your truth. Being alive is to live by exploring your power and moving to reach your dreams to discover your truth. While being vulnerable within can weaken you, being open about your vulnerability with loved ones, or even better with your counsellor, can clear your doubts, build trust, deepen connections, and make way for acceptance. Opening up about your confusion and doubt, and second-guessing your doubts — in other words, <u>doubting your doubts</u> — helps release the power of those negative beliefs. By speaking about your doubts out loud, you are not letting them fester in the shadows. In fact, finding the inner strength to battle doubts and uncertainties is necessary to build a personal sense of resiliency and confidence.

"Indecision, doubt and fear. The members of this unholy trio are closely related; where one is found, the other two are close at hand."

Napoleon Hill

Being a real human is to live with the adventures of love mixed with hurt, peace mixed with letting go, and success mixed with failure. To live is to pass through the tunnel of fears and doubts. Certainty comes when you pass through the doubt and are not anchored by it. When you allow yourself to be stuck on the dark side of the past and are afraid of what the future might bring, you are living with doubt at the present moment. On the other hand, by realizing your apprehension of the present moment, you become aware that you can choose to hang on to fear or to faith. Only then can you start to doubt your doubts, and gradually work your way toward reaching faith in yourself. The moment that you decide to let go of the doubt, you move in the direction of success; if you give in to doubt, you choose the road of failure. Everyone can become afraid of failure, but the biggest failure is to avoid deciding and to stay in doubt. As Virgil Thomson said,

"Try a thing you haven't done three times. Once, to get over the fear of doing it. Twice, to learn how to do it. And a third time to figure out whether you like it or not".

Doubt breeds fear, and fear breeds illusion. By illusion, I mean that you use an excuse to avoid triumphs. The path to confidence is to develop a strong vision that is bigger than the fear and the doubt. Doubt is like a betrayer inside us that, once allowed to grow, will passionately hurt and destroy our confidence. Therefore, the only thing that can really defeat fear is a strong vision and a burning desire for what you want; this will break the passivity that fear brings. As Nelson Mandela said,

"I learned that courage was not the absence of fear, but the triumph. The brave man is not he who does not feel afraid, but he who conquers that fear".

Doubt brings fear, and fear paralyzes you by making you over-analyze everything and become overly cautious to a fault. Over-analysis then becomes part of a vicious cycle that ends with fear, doubt, and depression. By being constantly doubtful and afraid, you become more passive and more concerned with fear than with success.

"Don't waste life in doubts and fears; spend yourself on the work before you, well assured that the right performance of this hour's duties will be the best preparation for the hours and ages that will follow it."
Ralph Waldo Emerson

Doubt builds a haunted house, and by conquering the doubt you build an empire. A miserable life is built on doubt and fear, and a happy life is built on confidence and the willingness to try. Our inner world builds our outer world; constant thoughts of doubt are destroyers of creativity while thoughts of confidence are facilitators of invention. The first invention that you can create with your confident thoughts is your personal life. The fabrics of conformity in your life are woven in rows and columns made of fears and doubts. Every time you pass through doubts and fears, you further build a part of your life, learn a new lesson in courage, develop a sense to see the unseen, and gain more faith in yourself.

You can conquer doubt by loving what you want more than your current comfort and status quo. When you love what you want and act upon it, all doubts melt away. We all have doubts and fears. Fear comes from a feeling of insecurity and sees everything from outside-in, instead of inside-out. When you see things from the outside-in, you see only what others might think, plus you only see what others want from you. When you start from the inside-out and seek your inner desires, then your doubts and fears are eliminated and all thoughts of insecurity will sink along with them.

When we find ourselves in a crisis, we are often afraid because we know that we have to sacrifice something. If we have faith, courage, and honor, we know that we will be letting go of something with lesser value and gaining something with higher value. To overcome doubts and fears, your dreams must be lofty enough. When you dream, and dream big, you climb mountains and each achievement prepares you for the next. If you can imagine yourself in a place where it is not safe to stay, but returning is not an option, you will choose to move forward. Learn to imagine yourself in that tight situation and you will learn to conquer your doubts because you won't have time for them. Leap over each fear and doubt, and soon you will reach the top of the mountain. You might be frightened, but you will also be filled with a wealth of blessings. Doubts and fears are part of life; they are the part that you have to let go of to be successful, otherwise you have to sacrifice your dreams.

Experiencing doubts and fears when approaching new experiences is completely natural. You can even consider doubts and fears as bitter at times and the spices of life at others. While spices cannot be eaten on their own, in moderation they are the seasoning that makes life experiences more complex, exciting, and worthwhile.

As you anchor yourself to faith in yourself and develop positive anticipations, your fears fade away. This makes victory more achievable. Successful people do not have the time or energy to dwell on doubts, because dwelling on doubts is the seed of being stuck. Giving power to doubts creates victims, not victors. In fact, you can create a vision of victory to hold yourself on course until you earn your faith in yourself. When you allow doubts to accumulate in your life, you allow obstacles to accumulate; therefore, you invest more of your energy on battling these obstacles than on building your dreamed life. When those doubts and fears are conquered, the victory will be even sweeter. Consequently, you will come out stronger than ever. While doubts and fears can be your worst enemies, once you pass through them they become your makers, shakers, movers, and builders.

Sometimes you don't even have to fight your doubts to gain control over them, rather it may be enough to simply acknowledge those doubts. Fear of failure can be seen as an examiner of your personality; it can help you prove to yourself that you have what it takes to see it through. If you view life as a series of lessons that you have to learn as you go, then the tests of doubts and fears turn into new levels of power and potential. As Zig Ziglar said,

> *"The best recipe for happiness and contentment I've seen is this: dig a big hole in the garden of your thoughts and put into it all your disillusions, disappointments, regrets, worries, troubles, doubts, and fears. Cover well with the earth of fruitfulness. Water it from the well of contentment. Sow on top the seeds of hope, courage, strength, patience, and love. Then when the time for gathering comes, may your harvest be a rich and fruitful one".*

To sum up, where there is doubt, there is no movement or motivation. When in doubt, you focus more on all that might go *wrong* than on what might go *right*. To be able to build confidence, you must learn to stop defending your doubts. Being doubtful is a habit that creates drama instead of dreams.

Now let's examine another potential negative habit of mind which may be holding you from reaching your desired level of confidence.

Chapter Six: Being Worried

"Worrying is carrying tomorrow's load with today's strength - carrying two days at once. It is moving into tomorrow ahead of time. Worrying doesn't empty tomorrow of its sorrow, it empties today of its strength".

Corrie Ten Boom

Worrying comes from concerns about the future. The absence of worrying, therefore, can be a sign of growth, understanding, and confidence. When you are bound to security and want to have control over your tomorrow, you lose power and awareness of your present. If you can let go of the negativities of yesterday and instead remember what you learned yesterday, then you can use your power to live just for today. As human beings, we are designed to be able to handle one day at the time. If you want to carry two days' worth of life events at a time, you will be fragile and lose your power.

Your power is only available to you today, and right now you do not have power over the past or the future. Worry can even be defined as being constantly afraid of the future. The future is supposed to be something joyful and exciting, and when you pull towards it you are not supposed to be afraid of it. Your dreams are in your future, as long as you sow their seeds today. With every thought, you are watering the seeds of your dreams; if all you do is fear and worry about what is to come, then you are poisoning your dreams. When you live for today, you are aware of how you are watering your dreams, but you can only do this if you let go of your worries.

When you live a life in which you are constantly worrying, you live a life without awareness. Worrying and awareness are the opposite sides of a coin. When you are aware of your time and being, you are free of worries. When you are at peace with the past and not worrying about what the future might hold, you can experience your optimal power. In other words, your power lies in your awareness and whether or not you are focused on the present.

When you live by your highest values, you are at peace and not worried; you are dancing to your own beat. If you do not like your situation in life, you have a choice: you can worry about it or you can do something about it. By being aware of the present, you have the power to do something about what the future brings. By being worried, you are thinking about the future and what is missing in your life.

If you have a burning desire for what you want to acquire, then your desire will be more than your worries. In that case, you don't need to worry about anything you lack, because your burning desire will win. As Zig Ziglar said,

"Worry is interest paid before it's due".

When all you can think of are 'what-ifs', you are after security and control; all that matters to you then is to survive, not thrive. You must leave the comfort of your security to be able to grow and, instead of thinking and feeling bad about the things that you cannot control, you must be concerned with what you can control. The cure for worry is very simple: get up and do something about what you want. Worrying drains your energy without adding anything useful to your life, because it requires lots of energy to worry and fight in your mind with unpleasant things and unpleasant people. As General Eisenhower said,

"Let's never waste a minute thinking about people we don't like".

Spend time, money, and energy on the things that are important to you. If you put your energy toward planning your future and working towards those plans, you are nourishing your dream. Spending time, money, and energy on worries shows that you *only* value worrying in your life because that is where you choose to invest your resources in.

By choosing to focus on worrying, you gradually kill your dreams, confidence, and concentration. When you are worried, your mind is scattered and so is your energy, and you cannot make sound decisions. By overcoming worry, you can make decisions, take action, and go further in life. We all have potential that we are not aware of; it is only after we overcome our eternal worries and act upon new possibilities that our potential start to come out. If only we had confidence that we could do something, instead of worrying about the 'what-ifs', we would be shocked by our own abilities. Everything in the world can change except the law of change itself. If we cannot even put our foot in the same creek twice because the current constantly carries water away, then how can we have certainty about our future? Why should we worry when we can be happy and confident?

As I will state in more detail later, happiness is an inside job; by being confident you can be happy and joyful, and capture the power of now and let go of your worrying about the future.

"A day of worry is more exhausting than a week of work."

John Lubbock

When you are inactive and passive, you do not do anything; therefore, you do not have any experience. When you do not have any experience, you do not have much knowledge; when you do not have much knowledge, you lack confidence. You do not have confidence when you constantly worry, because that is all you do.

Consequently, you are not in the process of becoming the person you aspire to be, because there is no time or energy left for doing so. It would help to say to yourself that after all, everything works the way it is meant to, whether I worry or not, so what is the point of worrying? The only thing that worrying does is kill confidence and poison dreams.

You must remind yourself that worrying only exists in the mind as an expression of human weaknesses. No matter how subtle the worry is, it is a weakness of our intellectual understanding of nature and of our own being. Any weakness of attitude becomes a weakness of character; it becomes a lack of power to act with courage.

Confidence is the willingness to get what you want. The first requirement for confidence is to develop the ability to focus and apply your mental plus physical energies to the problem at hand. That is the way to stop wasting your strength on worrying.

Spending time worrying is like trying to fill a pot with holes; it keeps you busy but you get nowhere. Remember that worrying is all about what may happen tomorrow, while you are living in today. Tomorrow is supposed to be bright, exciting, and inviting, but worrying makes it dark and scary. When you live in a state of constant worry, doubt, and fear, you limit yourself mentally and take the brightness, excitement, and invitation out of tomorrow. People often suffer more from their own negative thoughts than from actual reality. If you worry a lot about how you will perform on an upcoming test, you have already failed, because you practiced your worries instead of your skills. Worrying gets you nowhere. Worrying about things in the future that you cannot control is insanity, and worrying about the things that you can control is a waste of time and energy.

"Sorrow looks back, Worry looks around, Faith looks up."

Ralph Waldo Emerson

So, you have to conquer your worries to gain confidence, otherwise they get you nowhere and leave you exhausted. Next, let's examine another limiting habit of mind that must be curtailed.

Chapter Seven: Laying Blame

"A man can fail many times, but he isn't a failure until he begins to blame somebody else."

John Burrough

B-L-A-M-E can be thought of as an acronym for Being Lame And Miserable Evidently. Things can go (horribly) wrong from time to time in everyone's life, but what a person does after a problem has arisen, is what differentiate between individuals. If you want to grow and build confidence, do not blame anyone or anything for what you have been involved with. Making excuses about your shortcomings is a practice that makes you smaller than the situation. Although it might seem easier to blame someone else rather than take responsibility for own actions, easy always becomes difficult. When you are late and blame the traffic for it, you might feel some momentary relief but it won't help with your poor planning. Instead of putting your focus on blaming someone or something for your problem, put your focus on resolving the real issue; no one else is in charge of resolving your issues. You can never fix anything unless you take full responsibility and put yourself in charge of fixing it.

People who lack confidence constantly look for someone or something to lay the blame on, not knowing that people come into your life for a reason, and not just to be blamed by you.

"Never blame anyone in your life. Good people give you happiness. Bad people give you experience. Worst people give you a lesson. And the best people give you memories."

Zig Ziglar

Another reason you should not try to find someone to point finger at is that by blaming others you give them not only your energy and your power, but also the power over yourself. You do all of that by putting so much emphasis on them. A key to being a strong person is to accept wrongdoings without blaming, and to take responsibility to make positive changes and to facilitate your growth. Strong people ask themselves the right questions, such as 'how can I fix what has been my part or my responsibility?'.

There are ways to approach responsibility that work and ways that don't. When your focus is on the blame, the issue becomes all about *who did* wrong instead of *what went* wrong. Blame can turn the situation toward judgment and create unforgiveness. When blame is used to divert attention away from self, it also turns the attention away from a solution. Therefore, blaming is a waste of time and shows a lack of understanding of what is our fundamental responsibility. There are two ignored realities about responsibility; firstly, responsibility cannot be assigned after the fact, no matter how hard you might try to do so, and secondly, responsibility is always present, even if not acknowledged. When you start to realize facts about responsibility, you stop blaming. You begin focusing on your own role instead of ruling others, whether in action or abdication. When you try to find someone or something to blame, you over-analyze the problem and paralyze yourself inside the problem.

It is important to emphasize that I am not saying you should blame yourself. Some people, especially when they lose ground by making a critical error, replace blaming others with blaming themselves. *Blame is blame whether you place it on yourself or on others.* Blaming yourself turns into self-recrimination, self-judgment, and self-hatred. Blaming yourself for something is not the same as taking responsibility for it; in fact, blaming is a way to avoid taking responsibility. Because the focus of blame is to find fault, its objective is not to empower but rather to put a restrain on the power. Finding yourself or someone else guilty is not going to change, fix, or improve anything. In other words, blame brings blindness towards the issue at hand. The price you pay for blaming is losing your confidence, because you are not able to face your fear of being wrong. Next, we will explore another way of thinking that can rob you of confidence.

Chapter Eight: A Victim Mentality

"Don't Take Anything Personally. Nothing others do is because of you. What others say and do is a projection of their own reality, their own dream. When you are immune to the opinions and actions of others, you won't be the victim of needless suffering."

Don Miguel Ruiz

People with a victim mentality think bad things only happen to them. They feel like they are taking the fall for someone else and therefore have resentment towards life. Those with a victim mentality also feel that they have no power of choice. Consequently, they view life as a series of unfortunate events that just happen to them, while for other people things have been handed over to them on a silver platter. They compare their inner world to the outer world of others.

There will always be people in your life who treat you badly or unfairly, but I want to tell you that you can also view them as if they are in your life to make you healthier. If you remain angry at someone, you are giving space in your head to that same person; hence, you are giving them power over yourself. Sometimes, when you are really mad at someone and cannot let go, you are in fact sitting, eating, and living with them, because you think about them all the time. You may not realize at the time, but you are actually making your enemy your soulmate!

Happiness is an internal state of mind and does not depend on external conditions. When you constantly think about, argue with, and fight with people in your mind, you cannot be happy. The best revenge that you can get on people who have hurt you is to not spend even a minute thinking about them, and become a happy and successful person, instead. Getting knocked down and being hurt are realities of life. So, don't see yourself as a victim and don't hold grudges. Letting go will make you free; learn to move forward as a choice to free yourself.

Happiness being an inside job also means that how you think and what you think about are all that matters. Nothing — no positions or possessions — can make you happy. You make your future from the thoughts of today. If you have the attitude that today is the destination and believe that the power is here and now, then you will live victorious, not victimized. If you live from where you are, not from where you used to be or where you will be, then you harness your power. You become self-made rather than living with the regret of who you wanted to be. So, learn and practice to think of hope, confidence, love, and success. To believe this, you need to have courage.

Stop trying to change other people and 'improve' them. The results will be only a feeling of exhaustion. Changing other people can be like trying to create a hole in a stone using a cotton ball; it won't work and you only frustrate yourself. However, if you learn to put the same level of energy into the betterment of yourself, you will get tremendous results very quickly. If you learn to see someone who hurt you as someone who is there to teach you what is right and what is wrong, then you can even thank them when you do the right thing. The words of an ancient proverb reflect this same idea: "*Where did you learn your manners? From rude people*".

So, if you want to be confident you must learn to recognize the victim mentality in yourself, and try to free yourself from it as soon as you notice it creeping back into your thoughts. A victim mentality robs you of confidence and creates drama in your life.

The following chapter discusses another thinking habit to be avoided in order to be more confident.

Chapter Nine: Expectations

"What makes Earth feel like hell is our expectation that it should feel like heaven."

Chuck Palahniuk

There is confidence, and then there are unrealistic expectations. People with high expectations of other people and circumstances are usually concerned with results and feel bonded to the outcome. This makes them very fragile and rigid. All that matters to a person who is outcome-focused is the quantity of the results, not the quality of the energy and effort.

Strict expectations also bring a sense of entitlement. Expecting to be chosen to play every time you try, and win every time you play, makes you develop a sense of entitlement. You become angry and disappointed if you don't get chosen, or win, which normally happens a lot. **It may sound odd, but depending on the individual, sometimes winning is the worst thing that can happen to a person.** For example, if you take winning for granted and expect to win all the time, you might become a gambler. Expecting to win every time is a recipe for disaster because it sets you up for disappointment and eats up your confidence as you strive for success. When you don't meet your perceived expectations, you feel unsuccessful.

High expectations drain your confidence, and confidence is the ability you need to bring determination to proceed in executing a plan. Because confident people are perseverant, they have faith in their own efforts and do not judge the quality of the performance based on pre-set strict expectations, results, or outcomes.

Expectations allow you to leapfrog ahead in planning. While expectations can potentially be very useful in creating the results that you are envisioning, but at the same time they shrink your confidence if you do not leave any room for the unexpected. Strict expectations come from fear, and therefore make you very narrow-minded and this can affect your performance. While positive expectations and confidence are intertwined concepts, strict expectations become a judgment. The expectation to always win is an obstacle in your growth and development. It can hold you back from succeeding and becoming confident because you get consumed by what you get rather than who you become. Your whole purpose should instead be to become a better person not necessarily someone who wins every time.

You can think of strict expectations as judgments and demands that you place on your performance. As a result, expectations can bring fear of failure, create mental conditions that become an obstacle to excellent execution, and cause a great deal of anxiety. High expectations also rob you of joy and limit your potential.

To create a successful path, you must replace your expectations with 'anticipation' and a willingness to learn and grow. Having high expectations makes you sure that you must get what you are after, that you must win. You might say to yourself, "I practiced so hard, and all that matters is winning", but, in doing so, the effort and learning are forgotten. Because you place all the value in winning and none on the effort you put in, you will get depressed or angry if you don't win.

As indicated earlier, the difference between a successful and unsuccessful person can be determined by their response to setbacks. While anyone may fall on the way to reaching their goals, the successful person bounces back whereas the unsuccessful individual stays down, gives up, and claims failure.

Therefore, there is a difference between confidence and having an expectation of winning, although some see them as interconnected. Willpower brings confidence and is based on the strength of the belief in your ability, or how strongly you think you can continue to create the results that you are after. However, expectation brings a sense of entitlement.

Next, we will discuss another disempowering habit related to confidence.

Chapter Ten: Comparing Yourself to Others

"Success is not measured by what you do compared to what somebody else does. Success is measured by what you do compared to what you are capable of doing."

Zig Ziglar

Simply put, the easiest way to be miserable is to compare yourself to others. On the other hand, the greatest asset is knowing that the key to a happy and fulfilling future, is 'you'! The value you add to your life directly depends on how much value you *think* you have. Don't compare your inside with the outside of others. Everybody has their own struggles, and as long as you walk above the ground, you have your own pain and obstacles. **For every flaw that you have, you also have at least its equivalent in talent.** You must focus your attention on yourself to find your talents.

To 'be yourself' is the greatest gift you can give yourself; you actually insult yourself when you try to be someone else or like someone else. Comparing yourself to others is ignorance towards yourself, your unique gifts, and your unique talents. Whenever you compare yourself to others, you are oblivious to your own gifts and talents, and you waste them. Celebrate your uniqueness to nourish your skills and contributions. You are the most deserving person to be the star of your own story; if you compare yourself to others, you become merely the stepping stone, understudy, or stunt person in your own story. Comparing yourself to someone else gives them your power and allows them to use your energy to gain confidence at your expense. When you compare yourself to others, envy others, or criticize others in order to feel good about yourself, you are feeding the other person's confidence. This is nothing but a waste of your time and energy.

The most important concept to help free yourself from comparison is to learn that you are not better than anyone else AND that no one is better than you. People are all different; they are like different flowers in the garden of being. The only measure that you must care about is how much of your talents you use for your achievements. The only person you should compare yourself to is 'yourself' — who you used to be compared to who you are now.

Comparing yourself to other people is like telling yourself that your abilities are limited and you are a second-class citizen. Self-confident people don't waste time sizing themselves up and worrying about whether they measure up to everyone they meet. Insecure people constantly doubt their importance and, because of this, try to steal the spotlight and condemn others to prove their own worth. If you compare yourself to others, you put your energy and focus on others' importance and deny your own importance. Because you can only put your energy and focus on one thing at a time, your focus is either on your own magnificence or on denying your own worth by thinking others are better than you. Those who are not self-confident, only see the success of other people. Self-confident people, on the other hand, aren't worried about their perceived importance by others, because they draw their self-worth from within.

We are all different and unique in our own ways; therefore, by comparing yourself to others, you lose yourself. If you easily lose yourself, it means you don't have any genuine respect for yourself, then you cannot give genuine respect to others. You cannot give what you don't have for yourself. As a result, you hate people you think are better than you, and pity people whom you think are less than you. In fact, when you compare yourself to others, you are violent towards yourself and can be very cruel towards others.

If you try to be someone you think is better than you, or if you want to mock someone you think is less than you, then you kill all of your gifts of uniqueness.

Life is like a one-way street — there is no going back. The journey of life can be akin to driving on a busy multi-lane highway. When you compare yourself to others, it's as if you pay more attention to what the other cars all around you are doing than to the road ahead. Of course, you must be generally aware of your surroundings as you make your way toward your destination; but, if all you do is to focus on other cars, you can get distracted and cause an accident. In life, just as in driving, you must spend most of your time looking ahead, with only occasional glances to the back or sides to know where you are compared to where you have been and where you want to go. Treating driving lanes as racing lanes can also put you and others in danger, because your focus is on getting ahead of a particular rival car with little attention paid to other considerations. You are responsible for driving safely, which you can only do when you focus on the road ahead. You tend to drive toward what you look at; if you focus on the road ahead, you drive straight ahead; if you focus on anything on the sides, you unconsciously steer in that direction. This is true for life as well. When you focus on someone else, instead of yourself and your destination, you might not get to your destination at all. By observing the golden rules of driving, such as being mindful of the road ahead and keeping your distance from surrounding cars, you can enjoy the ride and scenery of life along the way. There will always be some drivers who do not observe their boundaries, but if you focus on your own driving, you can adjust to any situation.

One of the things you need to work on is your way out of comparison. Stop comparing yourself to other people, as it can poison your life. Your real job in the world is to be you. Comparing yourself to other people hurts you more than anything. In this universe, there is one of each of us; we are all unique in our talents and other characteristics, so celebrate your uniqueness. 'You' are not even your hair, skin, height, or other physical characteristics; your parts are not equal to your whole. You find yourself bit by bit through events in your life. Life events don't 'shape' you, they only 'reveal' you, and finding out what works for you and what doesn't is the most important part of your life. Even among the players of a given sport, each teammate has very different abilities and skills that makes them unique for their role in the game.

You get lost when comparing yourself to others, just as you discover your gifts and find your purpose when you try to be yourself. When you respect the fact that you are different, you have fewer fears that limit your potential. Start to act upon talents that you have, instead of dwelling on what others have or don't have. In your own world, prosper using your gifts, no matter what anybody says. What matters the most is what you think of yourself. Recognizing how comparing yourself to others limits your inner power, can help you avoid this pitfall and instead compare "yourself" only to "yourself" to tap into your power and to be confident.

Now let's talk about yet another way of thinking that can rob you of confidence.

Chapter Eleven: Being Judgmental

"You can't depend on your eyes when your imagination is out of focus."

Mark Twain

One of the main reasons that people are afraid of moving forward is their fear of being judged by others. Judgment makes people narrow-minded and kills their courage. A road filled with fear is dark and narrow, but to reach success you need a wide and open road. Judgment distorts your vision because you look at everything through limitations rather than seeing the truth. *When you judge someone, quite often that judgment is a projection of who you actually are; therefore, your judgement is likely truer for you than for the other person.* Think of it this way: if you have astigmatism, the whole world is not out of focus; it's your eyes that are out of focus. In other words, you see yourself in the other person when your perception is twisted.

Judgment is also a sign of lack of confidence and passion. You can either love or judge others: when there is judgment, there is no room for love; when there is no love, there is no freedom. Confident people have peace of mind and passion in their heart, and they don't pass judgment on others, because they know that everyone has something to offer. *Judge yourself and you see and hear your judgment everywhere, but start to accept yourself and you see and hear acceptance everywhere.*

Freedom comes from accepting the reality of seeing things as they are; through acceptance you can rise above judgments and limitations. The only thing that can make you free and above judgment is if you try to understand yourself, others, and the situations without the limitations of prejudgment. If you do this, you can never be judgmental.

When you lack confidence, you are judgmental and your mind is busy analyzing negativity instead of planning and creativity. Rather than focusing inward on their shortcomings, confident people focus beyond their limitations, which allows them to see all of the wonderful things that other people can bring to the table. They can also see their own contribution and praise themselves, as a result, they can also genuinely praise other people for their contributions. The problem with over-analyzing is that you doubt yourself and others, and then you start to see everyone and everything with judgment. When you start to see everything from a place of peace, you won't get stuck in negativity. To move forward, you must move away from judgment and only then will your imagination be aligned, open, and receptive to reality. Therefore, you will be open-minded with accurate vision.

As a confident person, you aren't afraid of being proven wrong, because when you move away from judgment, you free yourself from negativity and can move towards growth. Once this happens, you start to become courageous and achieve your potential. When there is judgment, the focus is on 'who' is right and who is wrong, rather than on 'what' is right. With judgment, the focus is on shortcomings rather than the truth. Self-assured people know what they are capable of and aren't threatened by being wrong. They do not see being wrong as a personal deficiency and instead see it as an opportunity to learn.

Lack of judgment creates a place for building relationships. Relationships become weakened when there is judgment, while lack of judgment is a magic invitation that shows the courage to be united and move forward to build a relationship.

Judging yourself is bad enough, but judging yourself through the eyes of others is even worse. You judge yourself by how capable you think you are, but you also judge others based on how capable you think they are and not how capable they actually are.

If you feel that you are undeserving of something that someone else has, this is a judgment that they don't deserve to have it either. Similarly, just because you didn't have the courage to ask for what you wanted, you pass judgment that others who had the courage to ask don't deserve to have it either. People kill each other's dreams through harsh judgments, sometimes even the dreams of their loved ones. Lack of judgment brings acceptance of reality, motivation, and love. It breeds inspiration in yourself and others.

> *"Minds are like parachutes-they only function when they are open."*
>
> Anonymous

Finally, judgment robs you of confidence because your energy is invested in fear and not courage. Judgment is a restriction with respect to living a full and confident life.

Now let's move on to discussing another bad habit of mind that weakens confidence.

Chapter Twelve: Being Jealous

"The jealous are troublesome to others, but a torment to themselves."

William Penn

When there is jealousy, there is no love. Hearts are generous when there is love, but are clogged and lack compassion when there is jealousy. Some people are not successful because they focus on the success of others rather than on their own successes. When you are jealous, you put the focus of your attention on the object of your jealousy. In a way, you give positive energy to that person at the expense of your own accomplishments. Because jealousy makes you eternally blind, not only you lose sight of your goals but also your own greatness. Jealous people don't make progress, nor do they see what they have. Jealousy destroys confidence like a fire in the willpower storehouse, burning the peace and purity of your talents.

When you are jealous of someone, you feel they are superior to you. Jealousy is one of the most negative emotions and an obstacle to your own progress. While confidence enables you to think you are able, jealousy makes you think that the other person is better than you. In other words, jealousy is a declaration of inferiority to others. When you are jealous of others, you prove how high you see the other person compared to yourself. In fact, in your mind, they are the star of your story and you are the pedestal on which they shine. You allow your spirit to soar when you stay away from jealousy because you see your own greatness, and that makes you confident.

Jealousy eats away at your trust in yourself. Jealousy is an obsession that you have towards someone else; it is very sticky in nature and stays as long as you allow it to. When you are jealous of someone, you overestimate their talents and underestimate yours, because you give your energy to them. You use your own power to feed them. Jealousy also puts distance between you and others, destroys your peace of mind, and makes you miserable.

Jealous people might be painful to others but they are worse with respect to their own life by filling it with suffering. As soon as the feeling of jealousy boils up in your life, remember to have faith in yourself, show confidence, and watch the jealousy evaporate. Confidence and jealousy are opposing qualities that cannot coexist.

Confident people are inspired by success in general, be it their own success or that of others. In contrast, jealous people are afraid of success, because they don't see their own success and are only busy focusing on the success of others. Because their victory is in pushing others down, jealous people see their own success as follows: 'if I can't have what I want, I can break others and watch them fail'. The reason jealous people think this way is that by being jealous, they think of themselves as much lower than others and believe that success is for others. By resenting the success of others, they create an image of inferiority for themselves. Therefore, while confidence breeds success, jealousy breeds failure.

So, jealousy robs confidence and drains the power and joy out of life; a life without joy is an empty life. By being aware of the destructive power of jealousy, you can avoid it at all costs to build confidence.

"It is not love that is blind, but jealousy."

Lawrence Durrell

CONCLUDING REMARKS FOR SECTION 2

Throughout this section, we talked about the 12 habits of mind that rob you of confidence. One or more of these limiting habits are common among people who lack confidence. You may relate to some of the discussed habits more so than others, but we all as human beings have, at least at some point in our lives, had personal experience with many of the preceding habits. Therefore, merely finding examples of past records of these limiting habits in your mind is not unusual. Rather, you want to make sure to take action if any of these negative habits of mind are currently persistent and dominant.

What is important is that, by being aware of these negative ways of thinking, you can be mindful of their presence, their potential harm, and not allow them to undermine your confidence. When you have an awareness of all of the potential negative ways of thinking, then you can more easily stop them and substitute them with positive habits of mind that will help build self-confidence and personal freedom.

In the next section, we will discuss the 12 positive habits of mind that can help you build self-confidence.

THE 12 POSITIVE HABITS OF MIND THAT BUILD CONFIDENCE

INTRODUCTION

Unless you fully understand your own true power as a person, you cannot come close to achieving total self-confidence. The degree to which you truly acknowledge your own uniqueness will determine your ability to free yourself from self-imposed limitations.

The only sure path towards improving your own understanding is through taking command of your own life. Once you gain total insight of who you are as a person and know your number one priority, then you are on the path to build confidence. For this to happen, you must examine your ways of thinking and look at the inside, rather than the outside to solve your problems. As Buddha said,

> "Be a lamp unto your own feet and do not seek outside yourself ".

Now let's examine the most important positive ways of thinking that can transition your life towards total self-confidence.

Chapter One: Believing in Yourself

"Man often becomes what he believes himself to be. If I keep on saying to myself that I cannot do a certain thing, it is possible that I may end by really becoming incapable of doing it. On the contrary, if I have the belief that I can do it, I shall surely acquire the capacity to do it even if I may not have it at the beginning."

Mahatma Gandhi

The first and most important step in building confidence is to start believing in yourself. This is because you are undoubtedly braver than you think you are, more talented than you know, and more capable than you imagine. Through self-belief, you can start to uncover your potential; and your potential is unlimited! The only person who can put limitations on you is *you*, and the only way you can stop limiting yourself is by being aware of what you are doing and having stronger beliefs about your capabilities. You can protect yourself from anyone and anything, but you can't protect yourself from *yourself*, if you are not aware of your negative thinking.

Confident people put all of their focus and attention on what they do. To build confidence, believe in yourself and demand 100% from yourself. When you trust in yourself, you become the greatest power in your life. When you have confidence in yourself, you know that you cannot demand it from anyone else. When you believe in yourself, you do better in whatever you do.

You need to have expectations from yourself in order to build your life. You enhance your confidence when you pour all of your mental, emotional, and physical energy into what you do. This will result in achieving more than what you thought possible and as a result, you start building trust in yourself. You build confidence by believing in yourself; having faith in yourself is the biggest gift you can give yourself. You can never demand from anyone else to believe in you; it is your job and your responsibility to believe in yourself.

When you acknowledge your capabilities, you are on the right path to building your confidence. By believing in your potential, you will expand your desire to give more than what you are supposed to. Believing in yourself makes you generous in all aspects of your life, and it is not just by giving away money. When you believe in yourself, you are inspired to devote everything you have to the task at hand. This will allow you to build confidence but also to feel more fulfilled in your daily life. Consequently, you will also develop a more compassionate attitude towards yourself and others, while noticing that you also have more courage to give than what you are paid to do. Doing more than you are asked will overflow into your future life as an investment in yourself. You may agree that making interest on your investments is better than making simple wages. Consequently, your productivity and achievements will increase, because now you believe in yourself. Every day, you will try to do a little more and a little better than the day before.

Your inner beliefs are strong entities that determine your life's road map and your behavior along the way. So be aware of what you choose to believe about yourself. You can easily harm yourself by having negative self-beliefs, so much so that at times, you may feel worse about yourself than you feel about any other person on Earth. But remember that *no one, except you, can make you feel good, just as no one, except you, can make you feel bad.* If you truly understand this concept, you will have all the power you will ever need.

If you pay attention, there are times when you may notice you are dragging yourself down, as if you were your own worst enemy. If this happens, stop and make a conscious decision not to pull yourself down any further and rather, continue along the positive path of believing in yourself and your unlimited potential again.

This belief in self can help you to grow. You must have a strong belief that you have gifts and talents; for that to happen, you must stop doubting yourself. More than anything else in the world, you need the courage to *forgive yourself, believe in yourself, and love yourself.*

There will always be obstacles, doubts, and setbacks in life. When these happen, try showing yourself how strong, resilient, and talented you are. View these barriers along your way as opportunities to practice being strong. When you are afraid, practice hope and when you have doubts, learn to have faith. Finding ways to show yourself how wise, strong, and gifted you are will make you believe in yourself again. Not believing in yourself is like giving others permission to steal your dreams. This is the time you become a sponge for cynicism, and others can easily influence you in a negative way. They may then project their own pessimistic beliefs about themselves onto you, and discourage you from pursuing your dreams. You may unknowingly accept their beliefs as yours. The most important thing is to trust in yourself. Your faith in yourself equals the whole world believing in you. The more you believe in yourself, the more believers you create. You can never trust in yourself and others if you do not believe in yourself.

As explained in the previous section, when you compare yourself to others, you give away your uniqueness, which is your power. Your power and confidence rely on you seeing your own uniqueness. In this universe, there is no other person just like you, and this uniqueness must be appreciated to become your source of power.

The belief about yourself is objective, rational, and where your willpower resides. A strong belief may be viewed as a gatekeeper who controls the access to your unlimited abilities. Your mindset monitors all of your actions, and your abilities will be determined by what you think you can do. When you have an "I can do" belief, your desires become your mission. If you believe that you can do it, then you allow yourself access to a treasure chest full of capabilities to make it happen. Therefore, the only gap between you and your goal is your trust in yourself.

Your self-belief is like a thermometer of your potential actions that shows how far you can go. All of the powers you ever need already lie within you, but it's your beliefs that determine your courage and determination to use them. You may think that the worst thing that can happen to you is not having an external support, but in fact the worst thing is not having your own internal support.

You may also think that you would have extraordinary opportunities if you were luckier, but in fact, only people with low confidence wait for opportunities to arrive; confident people create opportunities by turning the common into the extraordinary. The most distinctive quality of a highly confident person is a simple yet strong belief that they have *the ability to change their future by solely changing their attitude.*

There are no disabilities in people, because abilities are relative. For example, a person who lives at the North Pole must have different abilities than a person who lives in the Amazon. Both of these are very capable people but in very different ways. They may not be able to quickly adjust to living in one another's locale, but they are still very capable in the context of their environments.

If you have strong beliefs in yourself, then you can gain the ability to achieve your dreams along the way. As your experience expands, you would clearly see the impact of a positive outlook on your life. You would then realize why you are the only person who can change your life and no other person can do it for you. If you feel you are in a constant state of conflict and chaos, the only thing you have to do is decide to change your attitude.

Your belief also determines how well you perform at a task. Your belief at the beginning of a hard task, more than anything else, will affect the result. The interesting thing is this: 90% of what makes people different is just their view of events. A positive attitude makes the actions of confident people more effective and productive. Instead of thinking *why you cannot* do something, you must focus on *how you can*. One of the most important things that you can do is deal with your self-doubts, and "doubt your doubts" to be able to see your capabilities. It's only then that you can turn your potential into reality.

Highly confident people believe in their ability to achieve. Think about it: if you don't believe in yourself, why should anyone else put their faith in you? If your belief in yourself is not sealed and secure, you are prone to accept the doubts of others. If you allow other people's doubts about your own abilities to get into you, it can quickly deflate your confidence, and you are not going to be immune from others' negative perceptions of you.

The most important step in building confidence is to believe in yourself and believe in your strengths, not your weaknesses. Having a strong 'I can' belief about yourself can serve to magically turn your potential into reality. If you do not believe in yourself, you are likely to accept any negative opinion of yourself from others, making the opinion of others your reality; you become like a magnet for the negativity of others. On the other hand, when you have a strong belief in your abilities, you will not give up, ever. Strong self-beliefs make you an ambitious person who makes confident decisions, will not settle for a lesser version of self, and is destined for greatness!

In the following chapter, we will discuss another positive habit of mind which helps build high confidence.

Chapter Two: Defining Yourself

"Never be bullied into silence. Never allow yourself to be made a victim. Accept no one's definition of your life; define yourself."

Harvey Fierstein

Whatever you define yourself as, determines your actions. When you define yourself as a confident person, your actions become confident. That is why confidence manifests itself in the trust you have in your abilities. You must have the conviction and firm belief that you are born with a set of gifts, and you must strive to nourish those gifts to thrive. Define yourself from the view of love, not from the view of fear, because defining yourself based on fear is delusional.

The first step in defining yourself is to establish your responsibilities. What do you consider as being your most important responsibility in life? I believe the first and foremost responsibility for anyone should be to represent themselves in the best way they can. In other words, it is your responsibility to honor who you are as an individual, as well as your values, abilities, and talents. You must define yourself as someone who has even more abilities than you know. Some of your most prominent abilities must include a desire to learn non-stop, to have faith in your abilities, and to turn your potential into aptitude.

Your definitions of yourself express your aptitudes. Your aptitudes come from the awareness of who you are and what you can do. If you only define yourself based on your weaknesses, you will undermine your own strengths and hinder your skills. Instead, focus on what you are good at and what you are capable of, then use these experiences to mend your weaknesses. To borrow an example from sailing, in-your-face wind is part of the ocean of reality; you can't stop it or change its direction, but a confident sailor can use the power of the wind to navigate toward their destination regardless of its direction. Similarly, you build further confidence every time you apply yourself to use the in-your-face winds of life to your advantage.

To know your true definition, you need the courage to be real with yourself. For example, if you casually described something more extremely than how it really happened and someone called you a liar, you know that you might have exaggerated but not lied. When you know yourself, and are honest with yourself, you will not be bothered by the definitions of others. Use that criticism to better yourself by finding creative and positive ways to use your abilities; don't waste your time and energy being bothered by the opinions of others. If you indeed tend to exaggerate, maybe use that attribute to write great novels and screenplays. Because you know yourself, you understand that what someone tells you does not define you; rather, it is just their definition of you. You can either accept it or reject it. For you, it is merely feedback showing how you were perceived by that person.

When you judge another person, you do not and cannot define them; you can only define yourself. Similarly, do not accept anyone's misjudgment, insult, or threat against you as a truth about you. Take it as what it is, feedback. If you noticed someone shooting an arrow at you, you would take action by protecting yourself, putting distance between yourself and them, taking cover, etc., but you wouldn't knowingly let the arrow sink into your body. Then why would you not protect yourself and allow the arrows of other people's judgement hurt you?

Let the best definition of you be the accurate definition that you have created for yourself. Accepting a definition of yourself from someone else's point of view is like trying to taste a food based on someone else's liking. You must define yourself the way you would define a business: define your own brand, describe the services you provide, highlight things that are unique about your business, and focus on the value that you offer. Your business competitors can't define you. Everyone wants to know who you are and why you're here. You are your own unique brand and just like the best brands you know, you must define your own uniqueness and forever surprise people.

What brand of person do you want to be and what kind of star do you want to be in the movie of your life? If your identity is negotiable, then you define yourself as an anxious person. When you are with people, don't be their puppet. Be a person who has the ability to expand your reality beyond the level of your desire. Are you defining yourself as a creator of your own world or as a helpless creature of the world?

Your strongest link or your greatest ability can also be your biggest liability, if you do not know yourself. If you don't polish your ability, it can sometimes demolish you. To get to know yourself, you must be open-minded and work on yourself. When you work on your education and your skills, you create and define a career for yourself; but when you work on personal development, you expand your definition to your entire life. By knowing your own definition, you become the star of your own movie, not a stunt double, pretending to be someone else.

When you define yourself, you must know that you are indeed describing yourself to yourself first, not to others. You are finding your own truth, so strive to define yourself based on your own most important values. These values, outlooks, and definitions are to be viewed as constant areas of growth. As you learn more about yourself and the world every day, be ready to enthusiastically redefine yourself in light of new learning experiences. If you want to have more than what you currently have, then you must learn more, to have more, and to be more. As Randy Gage said,

"To manifest prosperity, you have to redefine yourself from a recipient to a co-creator. You have to stop looking for opportunities to present themselves and start creating them".

Identify yourself with positivity, and watch how the magic wand gathers up miracles with which you can become the star. Use the phrase 'I am smart' often, and see how you unconsciously become more willing and inclined to learn and grow. The majority of people, at least at some point, identify themselves with their shortcomings; over time they become comfortable in these shortcomings or, even worse, identify themselves using definitions provided by other people. Never use phrases such as 'I am lazy' or 'I am not loveable and no one wants to be with me'. Run away from all such negative self-definitions as you would run from wildfire. Instead, acknowledge your shortcomings as areas of improvement or things that you have to work on to be become the best version of yourself. Fostering confidence and your betterment can only happen if you first take responsibility for defining yourself.

You are the creator of your life, but you first must make the claim 'I am the creator and power of my life'.

Once you define yourself, and search for who you really are, you can tap in your powers by being aware of your own definition.

The following chapter explores another important habit of mind that can build confidence.

Chapter Three: Taking Responsibility

"If you take responsibility for yourslf you will develop a hunger to accomplish your dreams."

Les Brown

When you take responsibility, you take the most important step to changing things — guaranteed. Being responsible gives you the ability to be reliable and accountable, and gives you the power to respond. To be responsible doesn't mean to be at fault or blame yourself for failure. Highly confident people take ownership of and responsibility for their thoughts and actions. They are in charge and neither make excuses nor blame things outside of themselves. They do not give their power to other things, such as other drivers on the road or the traffic for being late to work. They don't allow the situation and their shortcomings to demolish them; instead, they work on their shortcomings to make changes to polish themselves. To become confident, see your limitations as areas for improvement, and take the time to keep on improving until you know you have done your best.

If the word 'responsibility' sounds like a serious matter, it's because it is. Responsibility is very different from a tug-of-war, placing blame, or finding fault. You must take responsibility mindfully to execute confidently. Putting effort into things over which you have control gives you power. If you take responsibility, you are in control; you are the mover and shaker that creates change. You are the CEO, president, the commander-in-chief of your own life. Being in the highest decision-making position for your own life means that you have the power and are also responsible for how you use your power.

Take control of your life by taking responsibility for your decisions. See yourself in the driver's seat of your life. When you feel you have the power and are the only person responsible for your own life, you become the creator of your life. Knowing that you are in charge of your life will make you calm, grounded, and confident. When you start to look at things differently with a renewed perception, things start to change. You will soon find that challenges in life become more manageable and there will be more flow in your life. It feels much better to be responsible than to be busy losing your strength in the blame game or the game of 'tag you're it'. Remember, being responsible is taking ownership of your action, be it good or bad. It is different than 'holding someone responsible' or 'finding fault with someone'.

Taking responsibility for whatever happened should provide some new and useful insight rather than distract from the solution, which is the result of blame. When you hold someone responsible, your emphasis is on 'hold' not on the 'responsibility'; your focus is on finding fault and blame. Taking responsibility, on the other hand, is a superior objective or path — it is all about accountability. Responsibility is a process, not the conclusion to a process. When something is assigned to you, it becomes your responsibility, making you want to take care of it, manage it, protect it, and make it successful. The most important factor to consider here is that responsibility cannot be assigned after the fact. In other words, responsibility is meaningful only in the present moment; it is meaningless in the past.

Blame comes in different shapes. When you use phrases such as 'to hold responsible', you are either blaming yourself or the other person. A better phrase to embrace is 'to accept responsibility'. It is best if you know beforehand what responsibilities are yours. For example, you can't say that it was your fault that you got angry last week; you can only learn from that experience to be proactive and not reactive. Blaming yourself is a 'path toward the problem', leading you to become stuck within the problem; if you focus on the blame, you cannot see the superior path. Keep in mind that your acceptance didn't bring your responsibility into existence at that moment — it was already present. Otherwise, it becomes a painful experience of blame if you take responsibility after the fact.

Accepting responsibility is not always easy nor does it provide instant pleasure. Taking responsibility makes you move toward the solution; therefore, it requires you to take action and requires you to work hard. Consider your responsibility for taking care of your pets or your back yard. It is not easy to make changes in your life routine, provide consistent care, or spend time and money to make sure your pet or back yard is well taken care of. However, you get to enjoy them when you do. Just like taking care of your pet or your yard, you must take responsibility for your own actions or your own life. Not taking responsibility, not taking your responsibilities seriously, or shifting your responsibility onto someone else can ruin the opportunity to enjoy the reward of being confident that you are in charge of your life.

When you take responsibility for your own life and actions, you still don't know where life is going to take you, but you will believe that life always happens for you, not to you. You will no longer think that you have bad luck or that bad things happen to you, because you see yourself as the creator of your own life. As Stephen Covey said,

"We all go through stages. Concerns about appearances, making good impressions, being popular, comparing yourself to others, having unbridled ambition, wanting to make money, striving to be recognized and noticed, and trying to establish yourself—all fade as your responsibilities and character grow".

In the next chapter, we will explore another habit of mind that helps you to build confidence.

Chapter Four: Dealing with Challenges

"When we are no longer able to change a situation, we are challenged to change ourselves".

Victor Frankl

When life throws you challenges, it is even more important to have faith in your abilities. Basically, you can either face the challenges that come your way and rise above them, or you can run and hide. As part of the process of transforming your potential into achievement, you have to through challenges and, if you choose to face them, you make growth happen. Once you grow in the face of a challenge, you witness positive change — that is a fundamental law of the universe. Only the law of change itself never changes. You may not like or want to face the challenges along the way, but you will still experience them and you will still go through changes, although it may not be the kind of positive change that is related to growth. Difficulties are a part of life and you grow your character by dealing with those hassles along the way. Life challenges either bring despair and depression or become an instrument to help you find your ultimate personal power. Challenges are the root of all creation.

What differentiates a confident person from an insecure person is how they face the challenges of life. Confident people use the predicaments as an opportunity to develop their aptitude and build more strength. Therefore, they never give up and conscientiously go after their objectives. Life is filled with obstacles, so develop a habit of facing them, taking action, and overcoming them. **Perhaps the most important qualities that help you go through the hardships of life are patience, empathy, and understanding.**

In fact, challenges are not merely limitations; they are opportunities to grow. Challenges are **the tools that make people grow**. A piece of coal cannot become a diamond unless it endures extreme pressure. Challenges are like steps that you encounter in life. You can't avoid them and you can't ignore them; you have to use them to either go up or go down. Going up is harder, takes more energy, and can be scary, but must occur before you can go on to the next step. You are confident when you are up for challenges, and being up for challenges means that you take action and have a "can do" attitude. What makes you confident is learning more about your abilities than your limitations, and preparing to take on challenges.

Being able to face challenges is a necessity for dynamic intellectual activity as well as for mental, physical, and spiritual growth. Shortages of complexities and challenges diminish the vast potential of every human being. By not being challenged, you become like an arm in a cast; you gradually lose strength and potential. *If there is no challenge, there is no chance to grow.*

Another tool you can use to face challenges is creating a deeper insight by developing a higher understanding of your responsibilities. As your understanding grows, so does your sense of responsibility; you learn to work not just for your own needs but also the needs of your family and society. Once you become bigger than the needs of your own life, you become fulfilled. That's the real meaning of **being altruistic.** Your growth continues as long as you continue to stand up to challenges. Your growth is like the growth of a tree, which first grows to the outmost of its own abilities before it can provide fruit or shade. That's the real meaning of life.

The challenges of life glorify you and add to your value. When you are a person of action, you choose to put the focus of your attention only on the objectives. The most significant sign of maturity is when you know that challenges are not obstacles. Instead, challenges are the wind that makes a tree grow longer roots and become stronger. Only when you are busy taking actions can you become bigger than the challenge; because taking action prevents you from overanalyzing the challenge and becoming paralyzed by it. Improved trust in yourself after being challenged is the prime prize for dealing with challenges. The heart of endurance is rooted in how many challenges you have gone through.

During a difficult experience, you may have a hundred reasons to stop, but if you can come up with a thousand reasons to continue, you will persist and endure. Confident people have endurance; they see obstacles, conflicts, and failures as part of the journey towards their goals. Once you develop the mindset to view obstacles as assets to be used as steps to go higher, you can turn your worst days into your best days of learning and growth.

No doubt, some people in your life will be harsh, but you can learn something from all of them. You can probably list all the people who have been or are still harsh with you and constantly challenge you. Instead of being angry at them, consider this: what if they have come into your life for a reason, to make you stronger. Paradoxically, it is often your best friends, mentors, or motivators who push you further in life and challenge you to be stronger. It is ironic, but those who you identify as being harsh with you, might actually be the ones who see the talent in you, even if you haven't seen it in yourself. However, it is also quite possible that some of those who are harsh with you may not be your friends, teachers, or mentors, and in fact you tend to identify them as your competitors, enemies, or just plain ignorant. Still, they are the harsh wind that makes your roots stronger, so be thankful for them as well. Take their messages and become the best version of yourself. Some of the people who hurt you the most are actually the ones that might nourish your biggest talent.

While our kind friends can help us in many ways, sometimes our enemies can provide us with the challenges and opportunities we require to develop the tolerance, patience, ambition, talents, and drive needed to succeed. Strive to view all of these challenges positively and as treasured life lessons that will bring you inner calmness, once you pass through them.

We only build resilience through challenges. As the famous proverb goes, what doesn't break you makes you stronger. Resilience is a skill that you acquire through the process of growth by going through hard times in life that requires courage to take action. You develop strength by facing the challenges of life. Between the challenges and taking actions is your "well of power", where you either choose to grow or just passively go through the change. Change is part of life; it is a natural process, but growth is the optional moment between the challenge and the action. Courage is something that you can't buy or develop by wishful thinking. You have to take action by choosing to face the challenges head on, in order to be rewarded with confidence and resiliency as a skill.

The more self-confidence you have, the more courage you have to take advantage of the opportunities presented to you. This is important because opportunities are limited. Therefore, be brave and take appropriate risks. Courage gives you the power to start new things, and confidence is the fuel to accomplish them fully. When you believe in yourself, you are not hesitant to initiate new plans; you know that you can be the pioneer of your own life, despite others' disagreement. Self-confident people dare to face challenges and put their opinions out there to see if they hold up. If their ideas do not hold up, then they still learn a lot from the times they were wrong. If you have an ability but don't have the courage and enthusiasm to use it, then that ability is wasted like a seed in a nylon bag — never given the opportunity to grow. You also need to have the courage to know that for every few steps forward you may need to take a step backwards. Taking these steps backward doesn't mean that you have failed; it means you had a learning experience.

"What is to give light must endure burning."

Victor Frankl

Embracing challenges is one of the most important steps in building confidence.

The following chapter will explore yet another great habit of mind that can help build confidence.

Chapter Five: Being Process-focused

"Strength does not come from winning. Your struggles develop your strengths. When you go through hardships and decide not to surrender, that is strength".

Arnold Schwarzenegger

As you become process-focused, you will only focus on finishing the task on hand. When you are filling a bucket with a small spoon, it can become frustrating but instead consider how every spoonful takes you closer to completing the task. Persistence is the character that you build on the journey to reach your goal.

To build confidence, eliminate restrictive expectations that are obstacles on your path to success, and instead focus on your effort to drive for excellence. When you focus on the process, you are making dots, and the dots are making a line, even if you don't realize it until you finish. Once you look back, you realize that each individual dot that you placed on the paper is contributing to making the line. There is no perfect dot, but there is only persistent effort that makes the line. Through this process, you will improve more and more, and the process makes you a better person by nurturing your talents. When you become more than who you were, everything else gets better. Enjoy your journey, because who you have become *is* the prize.

Heaven is a great reward, but it shouldn't make the value of life less important. The destination is important, but the journey is *everything*. When you reach the destination, it means that process of your journey is over and has come to an end. You may then realize that the journey has been the most powerful prize of all, not the destination. When you reach your destination, another journey may begin, and it's important to pay attention to the new journey. As Mike Dooley said,

> *"Impatience is a sign of hurrying; hurrying is a sign of worrying; worrying is a sign someone forgot time is on their side."*

If you are looking for the perfect moment, it is nothing other than the moment you find the meaning of life and can add value to your life as well as to the lives of others. All phases of life will end one day, so start new ones with a good spirit and open arms. Life is about taking actions and experimenting without fear. These actions and experiments will become experiences towards a fuller, richer life. In this way, each new phase of life becomes better and stronger than the last.

> *"Success is not a destination: It is a journey. The happiest people I know are those who are busy working toward specific objectives. The most bored and miserable people I know are those who are drifting along with no worthwhile objectives in mind".*
>
> Zig Ziglar

Let's take the example of taking a train ride. The most important things for you may be to enjoy the ride and be aware of where you are and where you are going. While it may be important for you to sit where you can see better to enjoy the scenery; if you become overly obsessed with the ideal seat on the train, then this obsession prevents you from enjoying the ride altogether. On the other hand, if you ignore the destination announcements, then even the best seat on the train won't matter if you miss your target station and end up at the wrong destination. You must know your objective; it is the clear objective that keeps you on the right path. The journey is the important part of the trip so be aware of your journey as well as your destination.

Another point to ponder is that, who you become in the process of reaching your objectives is the best part of the journey. If you are not in the process of becoming the person you want to be, you are automatically engaged in becoming the person you don't want to be. Once you have made a solid decision based on facts and due considerations, take action! Stop looking back over your shoulders and don't begin to reconsider, hesitate, worry, or retrace your steps. Otherwise, you lose yourself in the self-doubt that begets other doubts.

Continue on your journey; keep your eyes on the objectives and not on the problem. To build confidence, focus only on the next action that you can take at the present moment, instead of on the outcome, which might be unpredictable. Having clear objectives will help you concentrate on execution and drive for excellence, instead of putting an obstacle in front of yourself by focusing on the destination (outcome). Do your best in any given moment, and persistently work towards the target. The key to success is being able to see that an error is just another experience and is simply part of the process.

It is important to see life as a process, as opposed to solely focusing on the destination. If we appreciate the process of life, we can see life as a gift. Living by this understanding will make us confident and the living itself the prize.

Let's now move on to discussing another habit of mind to develop in order to build confidence.

Chapter Six: Being Goal-oriented

"Setting goals is the first step in turning the invisible into the visible."

Tony Robbins

When you set goals, you bring your talents together and assemble them to turn your aptitudes into reality. To build confidence, you must replace doubts by giving attention to your strengths. In the process of reaching for your goal and building confidence, you will also find your power in the process. One of the most significant ways to build confidence is to set goals and strive to reach them. You build confidence by being receptive to opportunities in your life and making it your mission to work towards them. If you don't set a goal for yourself, someone else will set it for you, and you will have to work towards their goal instead. As Napoleon Bonaparte said,

"I see only my objective — the obstacles must give way".

Having objectives makes you the person you wish to be; therefore, be careful what kinds of goals you set for yourself. If you set negative goals such as revenge, they are going to be costly because they drain your energy and undermine your own importance. On the other hand, when you set positive goals, the process will also nurture your own skills and talents. You will fill your life with the passion of achieving what you are after. If you have a goal, you can use the power of your collective resources to help you to achieve your dreams. When you realize your abilities and power, then you must set a goal to turn your potential into achievement. People casually give up their power when they don't see themselves as powerful.

Setting goals will also help you develop the abilities needed to reach what you want. Most people learn to either work towards what they want, or work for other people to help them reach their goals. When you don't have your own goals, you become the training wheel of someone else's bicycle. Being intensely focused on a specific goal means that your imagination is aligned with your desire. Determination will help you to grow and see that your goal is achievable, no matter how long the process takes. When you set your mind to a goal, the focus of your attention makes you more mentally and emotionally skilled, and you become a more sophisticated individual. At the same time, if the focus of your attention is on working towards the goal of another person, you become very skilled at following the dreams of others, and over time become naïve and less sophisticated in your mental and emotional abilities. The course of your actions is always moving you towards your destiny.

> *"The ultimate reason for setting goals is to entice you to become the person it takes to achieve them."*
>
> Jim Rohn

When your mission is very clear, your journey will be natural and spontaneous. You build confidence by realizing that you can achieve anything when you put your mind to it. By building confidence in this way, you will have the courage to be more ambitious and to dream of bigger goals. By having faith in your abilities and having the grit to make your wishes come true, you will know that only your effort can fill the gap between you and your dream.

Everybody is moving towards something. If you are goal-oriented, your movement goes towards your goals. If you don't have a goal, you might actually be working against yourself by passing up opportunities and catering to the goals of other people's lives.

In the large scheme of life, goals are like steps; one goal leads to the next. The main goal in your life is to be a better version of you. If, despite all of the ups and downs of life, you carry on towards this main goal, then you have made a real achievement!

*A goal without a plan and a due date is only a wis*h. Life is a matter of choice and awareness, not chance or luck. By setting goals, you are moving towards a meaningful destiny. When you set a thorough goal, it is as if you are halfway toward achieving it; the other half is in your actions. By having strong reasons for wanting to achieve your goal, you will figure out 'the how'. Setting a goal is the best indicator that you indeed know in which direction you want to go. It is the light that shows you the way, not the way itself. When you set a goal, who you become along the way is the greatest reward that you get.

The goal of a successful trader is to make the best trades. Money is secondary. One of the biggest elements in success is that you know where you are heading. When you have this realization, the awareness that you gain every step of the way is the greatest prize, because you will not be lost and you will know where you are heading. A major reason for setting a goal is what it will make of you, because by setting a goal you wish for who you want to be. Then by your own action you can accomplish what you wish for. The real trophy is what all of this makes of you. Who you become is the prize, not reaching the goal. The goals are the sparks of joy in your life because they make your journey more meaningful.

> *"People think focus means saying yes to the thing you've got to focus on. But that's not what it means at all. It means saying no to the hundred other good ideas that there are. You have to pick carefully. I'm actually as proud of the things we haven't done as the things I have done."*
>
> Steve Jobs

Indeed, wherever your focus goes, your energy flows. People who are successful have focused on success and have prospered mentally because they put their center of attention on progress rather than on what didn't work. Confident people put the focus of their attention on their goals instead of the results, while anxious people focus their attention on their doubts and weaknesses. Healthy people concentrate on their health, while unhealthy people focus on illness. Rich people focus their attention on profits, while poor people focus on losses. Happy people focus their attention on joy, while miserable people focus on calamity. Smart people focus their attention on learning, while ignorant people focus on difficulties. Whatever you are looking for, you will find.

When you become clear about what you want in the grand scheme of life, there isn't anything you can't accomplish. One of the great powers that will make a shift in your life is having a clear sense of what you want. Having a clear vision is next to having confidence. The first element in building confidence is to know what you want, and the clarity of what you want is a stepping stone in building confidence. Discover *what* you want first; then, by clarifying *why* you want it, you will create a path to get there.

It is not your "ability", but your "clarity", that builds confidence. When you ask confident people if they can do something, they have an attitude of *"no problem, I can do it"*. The problem isn't your abilities, it's what you think about your abilities. Perhaps who you think you are is twisted, and not who you really are. Confidence is the beginning of creating a self-awareness of what are you capable of and the person you want to be. Getting to know yourself and what you are capable of is important for turning abilities into achievements. As life goes on, be the learner, and learn from each situation.

After setting a clear goal, the only condition is that you work towards your dream. Consequently, what lies between you and your dream is the amount of effort you are investing towards it. You must first know what you want, and then have a very strong reason as to why you want it. Having the strong reason not only helps you keep going but also helps you figure out the how.

As the old saying goes, "when there's a will there's a way". Once you know what you want — the first link in the chain of clarity — then you must be very clear why you want it, and this becomes the second link in the chain of clarity.

> *"If you want to be happy, set a goal that commands your thoughts, liberates your energy, and inspires your hopes."*
>
> Andrew Carnegie

Clarity helps to align your imagination with your focus. The reasons you have for what you want make up the energy that you need to continue. Be sure not to get stuck on the "how", because the "how" is secondary to your main goal. You can never be sure as to how you will reach your goals. *The how is not your job; all you have to do is be very clear about what you want to achieve.* The planning becomes clear when you become clear about what you want and why you want it. If you put your focus on the how, you will become anxious, stuck, and may not even take the first step. However, if you become very clear with respect to what you want, you become excited and take the first step towards your goal. As Lao Tzu said,

> *"A journey of a thousand miles begins with a single step".*

The path of purpose is to become crystal clear about what you want in the process of life, so you can take your journey to reach your purpose. Clarity and being on the path of purpose build confidence. As mentioned earlier, even if a confident person can't reach their goal after a few tries, their way of thinking and their effort never die.

Confidence means you trust in your abilities and are willing to continue until you reach your goals. For the confident person, it's a matter of when, not if. For confident people, there is no such thing as failure because to them F-A-I-L signifies First-Attempt-In- Learning. For them, even getting one good result every ten tries is enough to be a great success! Confident people are "go-getters".

As Napoleon Hill said,

> *"Victory is always possible for the person who refuses to stop fighting".*

Moreover, your determination to take action is what determines your desired outcome. Confidence can be viewed as a combination of steps that you take to reach your destination. There will be falls over and over as you make your way towards your destination, but a big enough reason for what you want provides infinite fuel to help you reach your target.

Now let's move on to talking about another key step in building confidence.

Chapter Seven: Keeping Track

"On our track to success, we have to fight the tendency to look at others and see how far they've come. The only thing that counts is how we use the potential we possess and that we run our race to the best of our abilities."

Denis Waitley

Goal-oriented people working on a project keep a record of the tasks they do every day so that the next day they can build upon the previous day. To build high confidence, you should also keep track of the positive actions you take every day. If you keep a record of your success, you are more likely to achieve further success. The key here is knowing what you have done or achieved up to this moment. Don't worry too much about what was on your to-do list, but keep track of what you actually did.

When you keep track of your progress, you have more willingness to see obstacles in your way in a positive light. Seeing these obstacles allows you to see the pressure as only making you stronger. You will see that obstacles are, in fact, part of the process and are what make your limitations assets instead of liabilities. If you really think about it, everything is an opportunity for growth. At the end of the day, you can tally up your actions and ask, 'What are the things I have done today?' or, better yet, *'What are the things that I have done well today? And how can I make them better?'*

You build confidence through the things that you have done well, and by giving yourself credit for the effort that you put in. Thinking about the good memories and feeling good about the obstacles you overcame help you to build pride in yourself. Give yourself credit for what you have done and appreciate what you have learned and earned. This will also help you gain perseverance to go after what you want.

Trust that you are not alone in the world, and that there is always someone, or some source of power, with you. With this trust, your love towards yourself will start to grow. When you have unconditional love, then love starts to flow without effort from the depth of your being. When a baby starts to stand up or walk for the first time, they get excited and may even clap for themselves; in a way, they give themselves credit. When others clap for the novice toddler, then they also get to experience what it means to receive credit from others. The credit doesn't mean anything if the baby hadn't given himself/herself credit first. If they didn't feel they were doing something extraordinary, they probably wouldn't have gathered the courage to continue. Going forward, this sense of achievement helps them build upon the confidence to do other new things. Later in life, most people forget to celebrate their own achievements. When I ask people in my office what they like about themselves, sometimes it takes them a while to think of something to say.

The past can be a school of learning opportunities; it can be your asset to a wealth of knowledge if you want to learn from it, but it can also be your liability if you want to have regrets and not see the lessons. You have done many things that have worked for you, and it's important to know what you applied as a strategy that worked in the past, because the same may also work in the future. You probably have also made mistakes, but you must see the mistakes as experiences and learn from them to make better choices in the future. If you learn from the past, you can create a better future. So, you have to give yourself recognition for what you did well and learn from what didn't work for you.

Even though it's rewarding to reach your goals, do not try to measure or judge your track record based on others. You must put your focus on *yourself* during the action, because if you put your focus on your actions, your energy is focused on the process. Wait until after the process ends to reflect and evaluate your performance. Your experience could be the best learning opportunity if you take your time and reflect on it.

> *"Thankfulness is the beginning of gratitude. Gratitude is the completion of thankfulness. Thankfulness may consist merely of words. Gratitude is shown in acts."*
> Henri Frederic Amiel

Keeping track of what you have and what you have done is key to changing the direction of your life and making a fertile soil for cultivating the life that you desire. You must learn to say thank you and embrace what you receive with joy, act thankfully, and find the courage to ask for more.

Keeping a record of your achievements also means you know what you want, and can find what you are looking for more often. When you have an attitude of appreciation, you make your life a beautiful garden in which to cultivate your dreams. If you are humble, grateful, and aware of what is growing in your garden of life, you are on the right track for success. For instance, when you teach your kids about appreciation by saying thank you to them whenever they do something for you, this sense of appreciation encourages them to do more and become inspired to achieve greater things. You can nurture the best in your kids or anyone else by being appreciative and encouraging. The same philosophy applies to your own life; be humble to be able to receive, have appreciation for the things you have received, and welcome what you have not yet received.

Keeping a record means you acknowledge and understand what you already have and what you want, and that you are ready to receive more of what makes you happy. This habit of mind creates positive emotions; it indicates that you have understood what has worked for you, and what hasn't worked for you. As Dalai Lama said,

"The roots of all goodness lie in the soil of appreciation for goodness".

To this, let's add that in any given moment you can choose how to live your life. You can be aware and happy and appreciate what you have, or you can be ignorant, indifferent, or disappointed about what you do not have. You can complain that the cup is half empty or you can be grateful that the cup is half full and believe that it is refillable.

You show mental poverty if you ignore what you have. Having a habit of keeping track of what you did and what you have is good energy to deposit into your own life account. A wise man once told me to be grateful if you have a table, yet know that you can ask for a bigger table. The same is also true of behaviors and talents; if you like any of your talents, be grateful for it and try to use that to make your other talents greater. What you appreciate now will have a snowball effect in your life.

Appreciation creates healthy emotions and is one of the highest states of mind; it is part of the requirements of a happy life. Being happy is not just an absence of sadness or problems; it is keeping track of what you already have. Being grateful also makes you content, because when you are appreciative, greed disappears and abundance appears. The habit of knowing what you have and what you have done is a process of mental tuning which helps you find harmony in your life.

Now let's talk about the next habit of mind which can be acquired or nourished to become more confident.

Chapter Eight: Positive Anticipation

"Anticipation is the ultimate power. Losers react; leaders anticipate." –

Tony Robbins

When someone wonders about a sure way to build confidence, the answer can sometimes be as simple as finding joy in the things that they do every day. Enjoying the moment and having positive anticipation shape your experiences in a positive way. For example, when you can find enjoyment in winters, the cold of the season becomes a reason to play hockey. Your anticipation makes your experience enjoyable, and this becomes a continuous cycle. Use every experience in the past as a learning opportunity, be it good or bad. The past shows you how far you have come. You can go further with positive anticipation to learn better skill sets. Accomplishments breed accomplishments only when you have positive anticipation.

You are a valuable person who does many good things in the world. Open your mind, your eyes, your soul, and your arms to the marvelous gift that today brings. Accept the existence of today and remember that yesterday is past and you haven't yet met tomorrow. You have lots of great things to offer yourself, others, and the world. Learning new things only happens when you have positive anticipation. You grow and contribute even more to the world and others as a result of this attitude. Trust in the fact that you are not the first person to experience doubt and uncertainty, and that you certainly won't be the last. Everyone — even the most successful people in the world — at times experience feelings of despair and fear of 'not being good enough'. This simple fact of knowing that you are not alone can help those feelings dissipate, and allow you to bounce back from bad days and disappointments.

When you are doing something that is part of a larger goal, you might not realize your progress until you take a step back to see where you are within the bigger picture. Once you notice your progress, make sure that you appreciate, acknowledge, and admire your own effort. Live in the moment and celebrate every shining moment of your life.

For people with positive anticipation, there is no such thing as a dead end: they always find a way. Put differently, in their view the word END stands for Effort-Never-Dies. They will do more than what is asked, and will see everything as an opportunity to learn. When there is positive anticipation, the person observes the process and waits for something good to happen. Therefore, positive anticipation feeds determination. For example, when you anticipate the positive, you see everything as a reason for you to get closer to your goal and you have courage to continue towards your goal. Positive anticipation also gives you the energy to take action. As another example, when you anticipate that your kids will learn and grow from all of the things that you do for them, you are willing to take any and all actions towards that goal. The other benefit of positive anticipation is that you have the confidence to be proactive, thus giving energy to your effort and execution. Being proactive means you pause, think, and then act in accordance with your positive attitude.

As indicated earlier, anticipation is very different from expectation. Expectations are based on logical planning, which restricts flexibility. Expectations also set the outcome firmly from the beginning, and failure to meet expectations brings huge discouragement. With positive anticipation, there is the strength of resilience because it gives you the grit to adopt to changes in planning or execution. Positive anticipation gives you the courage to continue, while expectations can be disappointing. For example, when you think that you must win easily, it becomes an expectation, and as soon as you face any obstacle you will give up. Some people have lots of potential but seldom achieve anything significant because they expected to reach their goal without any obstacles. Therefore, they give up on their dreams as soon as they meet any serious obstacle. In contrast, Steve Jobs, who got fired from his own company, kept going because he saw it as a learning step towards his goal of changing the world. What kept him going was his positive anticipation towards his dream.

To give you another example of the difference between anticipation and expectation, imagine that you want to learn a new language. You can't expect that by only learning the alphabet or a few words you will be able to understand or speak the new language. Even if you expect that by learning a few hundred words you will be fluent in the new language, your expectations set you up for disappointment and may even kill your motivation to learn more. However, when you have positive anticipation that you will eventually learn the new language, then you will continue your journey until you indeed master the language. As Helen Keller said,

"Optimism is the faith that leads to achievement. Nothing can be done without hope and confidence".

Positive anticipation allows you to be available for opportunities and open yourself up to possibilities you couldn't even imagine. Believing that "effort never dies" will help you through a thousand tries to achieve your goal, if your goal is worthwhile and you are willing to take action towards it. When you have faith in your abilities and have positive anticipation, you know that sometimes you have to change direction because you realize there is a better way to get there, or perhaps an even bigger opportunity presents itself.

People with positive anticipation are not after a specific outcome, so they can just be prepared and plan well for achieving results. Both success and failure require planning, but one is based on positive anticipation while the other is based on expectations.

There is neither success nor failure without prior planning/anticipation. In positive anticipation, the motto is that if one door closes, then it must have been for your protection and a bigger door of abundance and prosperity will open elsewhere.

You might face obstacles during the process, but the key is to bounce back quickly and learn how to climb better until you reach the top/goal. When your level of confidence is high, then you truly believe "effort never dies". This affects the willingness to continue with no restrictions, and the motivation to continue remains.

With positive anticipation, you know that you will eventually reach your goals, so you faithfully move towards your goals, but without any rigid plans, because rigid planning can create obstacles to your willingness to continue. When you start to develop positive anticipation, you maintain your effort.

> *"There is no elevator to success; you have to take the stairs."*
>
> Zig Ziglar

Positive anticipation is necessary to build the confidence that leads to success. In the next chapter, we will explore how to use another positive habit of mind to build more confidence.

Chapter Nine: Open-mindedness

"Anyone who stops learning is old — whether this happens at twenty or at eighty. Anyone who keeps on learning not only remains young but becomes constantly more valuable — regardless of physical capacity."

Henry Ford

Confident people are open-minded in how they live their lives. This means that their mind is open to all the possibilities to learn and grow. They are open-minded to examine their mental habits, and this makes them the opposite of narrow-minded people. Open-minded people constantly adopt new positive habits, and see life as an evolving process of growth and expansion. They have high expectations of themselves; whatever they work on, they do their best. They find that their gifts and talents become more fruitful, because these gifts and talents become more than themselves. In this way, they can contribute to others, and this contribution makes them feel fulfilled.

Confident people are curious and have a burning desire to learn; therefore, they have an open mind to adapt and explore new ways of doing things. If you do your best, you are opening up space for your talents and gifts that will, in turn, make room and a place for you. Consequently, by doing your best throughout the process of life, you find your gifts and talents and can bring them out and let them grow. Confident people knowingly or unknowingly apply this formula in their lives: doing the best at whatever you do is what leads to great rewards in your life.

Confidence helps people welcome opportunities to grow and move towards a raise or a promotion; confidence results in higher positions and better jobs. Confident people are thirsty to learn, not only in terms of intellectual growth but also emotional growth and maturity. In fact, it is their open-mindedness that helps them become masters of their emotions and judgments.

Low-confidence people have a habit of putting demands and expectations on others. They do not put all of their energy into what they do, and as a result they live a life of mediocrity. They are hesitant to give all of their energy towards their own goals and dreams and instead long for the life of others. As a result, low-confidence people usually have poorer performance, and are narrow-minded and judgmental. Low-confidence people justify their poor performance with the excuse of not having a good job, and saying they would do their best only if they had a better job. It is exactly this poor attitude that causes them to end up in lower-level jobs in the first place.

The process of life is about moving, and since life is complex and involves many choices, it requires moving actively. Moving inactively downstream is only for things that are aging, fading, and diminishing. You must swim upstream through the river of life like an alive fish, because only dead or dying fish simply go with the current. The upstream life is where you are aware, open-minded, and make choices consciously.

To give an example, you must actively take care of yourself, your house, and your garden on a regular basis. If you don't, your health can be compromised, your house becomes filthy, and your garden becomes overgrown with weeds. When you create a set of positive habits to take care of those things, you have set the stage for your good health, your clean house, and a well-groomed garden. When are open-minded enough to allow the development of positive habits, your energy is flowing; without positive habits you may be wasting your energy. This is because, sometimes 90% of your energy will be consumed by the 10% of habits in your life. So, if those habits are the unproductive ones, then most of your energy is going to waste. For example, when you have a seemingly small bad habit of letting yourself to have a messy home, that mess can spreads through your life and becomes your normal way of being. That is why confident people are open-minded and receptive to what life has to offer, because they put all that they have into what they do.

Another thing that makes an open-minded person different from a narrow-minded one is that the open-minded person is constantly renewing their old habits. Imagine your collection of old habits as the water in a very large tank of live fish that is cemented to the ground. You cannot completely drain the tank or tip it over to quickly change the water. However, you can gradually add fresh water while taking the dirty water out. You must keep replacing the water until the whole tank's water is renewed. You must also continue adding new water to maintain its cleanliness. The real magic of new water is that the ecosystem of the tank improves. Using the same analogy, new disciplines and habits will cause you to improve your thinking. The most important point here is that changing a bad habit requires that you replace it with some new and better habits. If today you decided to learn to draw, attend dance lessons, pick up a book, start living in the moment, spend more time with loved ones, or any other positive change, then you can celebrate this day as the start of a new you. Once you experience the joy of enriching your life, one small habit at a time, you will be hooked and start to replace all of your negative or limiting habits with positive or empowering ones.

Everybody is longing to have more or to be more. Only confident people reach where they want to be and expand their lives. Why? The real reason for being open-minded is to be aware of any part of your life that does not work for you, not because you did not have enthusiasm but because you did not have the open-mindedness to embrace change. Open-mindedness brings awareness that you have a choice to make any change a process of growth. Change is part of life but growth is optional. Nothing stays the same forever. In fact, we all have some patterns of thinking that do not work for us. There is a myth that all we need is motivation to reach where we want to go in life, but this old way of thinking doesn't work. By relying solely on motivation, we are closing our mind to change and further growth. If you do not get the results that you want, you may want to try a new lens to gain a new perspective. The new perspective requires you to be open-minded.

The narrow-minded part of us may want to stay with familiarity and always go back to what we know. Because change is scary and requires a lot of conscious effort, we justify the familiarity because it is safe to stay the same. When all you want is safety and comfort, then the safety becomes your limitation. A narrow-minded person has a narrow and limited life. In other words, to be safe means that you end up sorry. The irony is that "easy" is actually hard, and "hard" is actually easy. For instance, a teenager who wants an easy way out and drops out of high school and then end up having to work hard for rest of their life. On the other hand, a student who accepts the challenge of schooling and works hard will more likely end up with a professional job. Acquiring new habits requires you to have an open mind. It is difficult, but when a new habit starts to work, the benefits begin to appear.

Confidence requires having an open mind. The mind is like a parachute; it is most useful when it is open, while there is nothing live-saving about a parachute that only remains closed. When you have confidence, your mind is open like a parachute and wants to explore what you can learn in any situation. An open mind is therefore key. We are all capable of healing ourselves and the key to healing is to have an open mind, and this is possible by changing a few habits. It is an open mind that allows us to see new possibilities and also makes us able to apply new ideas. We all have the ability to be open-minded. We can also choose what we want to be open-minded towards — either growth or regression — and it's that choice that makes us different. If we are open-minded towards positive things, we are able to learn and grow. The great benefit of being open-mindedness is growth. It is not our abilities that make for a great life; it is our open-mindedness that makes us available for opportunities.

Therefore, having an open mind is one of the most important habits of mind in building confidence. Open-mindedness is the ability that you can bring to living a good life. It helps you feel alive and powerful to continue on the path of growth. To change your life, you must be first open-minded to change your thinking habits. It is important to have an open mind to build confidence as this ability helps you get up when you fall down on your journey. In the next chapter, let's explore the next positive habit which helps build confidence.

Chapter Ten: Being a Leader

> *"A true leader has the confidence to stand alone, the courage to make tough decisions, and the compassion to listen to the needs of others. He does not set out to be a leader but becomes one by the equality of his actions and the integrity of his intent."*
>
> Douglas MacArthur

The true leader has passion and strives for excellence. Leadership is not about position or control; it is about making the best out of any situation or everything. Leaders not only know what they want, why they want it, and how to get it, but they also show others how to do the same thing by nurturing their own potential as well as the potential of others. The power of anticipation and inspiration are what make a true leader. As Carl W. Buehner said,

> *"People might forget what you said and what you did, but they will remember how they felt with you."*

People feel passionate for the vision of a leader. Life is filled with challenges and your abilities will be tested, but if you nourish your abilities through these challenges they will reveal the real you. People are attracted to leaders not because of their power but because they get empowered by them. Your personality or personal-reality will be created by the ups and downs of life: those challenges reveal who you are. Being able to steer your behaviors is to be able to make a change by choice, grow, and shape a new way of life. To have a chance to create change, you must advance change and direct it towards growth, take risks, and accept responsibility for making change happen.

True leaders grow towards being a better version of themselves: they are kind but not naïve, strong but not rude, thoughtful but not shy, brave but not bully, confident but not arrogant, vulnerable but not manipulative, and humorous but not absurd. A leader shapes a life that advances changes, innovates, resolves conflicts, and creates solutions to problems. A leader must be kind enough to relate to others, wise enough to have vision for others, flexible enough to be able to adopt changes, and humble enough to laugh with but not at others.

A leader looks beyond the problem and can find the best ingredients available to make the greatest meal. Leaders can improvise and expand to be more, to have more, and to do more for themselves and others. Leaders stand up during times of challenge, and reveal themselves in times of trial, not at times of comfort. Leaders are not 'know-it-all's' and seek the knowledge of others when they need advice. No leader can have all the answers, and a real leader knows that. Leaders do not tell others what to do and do not need others to tell them what to do. At the same time, they have the power to show vulnerability to ask for help and guidance. When a leader is present, they are the center of inspiration and people are inspired to be more, to do more, and to have more. As Eleanor Roosevelt said,

> *"A good leader inspires people to have confidence in the leader; a great leader inspires people to have confidence in themselves".*

In other words, the leader creates more leaders and elevates people from being followers to being leaders. Because leaders see leadership as a responsibility and not a position of advantage, they find ways to inspire their frontline people, to challenge them to change, and to make them resourceful. Leaders have personalities that make those around them feel like somebody rather than like nobody. Leaders train other coaches, teachers, and facilitators. A boss drives people; a leader coaches them. A boss depends on jurisdiction; a leader counts on good will. A boss deploys fear; a leader inspires passion. A boss demonstrates individualism and the hierarchy of power; a leader invites cooperation and demonstrates the power of "us". A boss facilitates blame for any breakdowns; a leader turns the breakdown into a breakthrough. A boss commands "GO"; a leader says "Let's GO!". A real leader knows that people who are on the frontline can offer the best solutions about how to address challenges.

You can inspire anybody to do anything, but no one can make you do anything. The only thing that you can do is influence others. You know you are a leader if you are a positive influence and a breath of fresh air that nurtures the potential of others. Good leaders help people turn their abilities into creations.

Life is about equality when you are leading; you have to learn to direct your own life and not be the follower of others to fulfill your potential. When you have good leadership skills, your mood is not at the mercy of the approval of others and you inspire yourself. Change how you define leadership, and you change how you run your life. Now let's move on to discussing another important positive habit.

Chapter Eleven: Self-improvement

"Teamwork is the ability to work together toward a common vision. The ability to direct individual accomplishments toward organizational objectives. It is the fuel that allows common people to attain uncommon results."

Andrew Carnegie

If you are looking for a magic wand to change your life, it must be self-improvement. To improve yourself from where you are now and reach where you want to be, you need to be open to working on yourself. The common denominator amongst successful people is working hard on everything but working even harder on improving themselves. Working on self is more challenging than any other work. Education can help you develop critical thinking, and continuing that education teaches you not to be critical towards yourself or others. School or formal education will get you a job, but working on yourself and educating yourself on interpersonal relationships will help you nourish your talents to create wealth, knowledge, and wisdom.

We all need each other, because you can never get anywhere as an army of one. Each of us is great at some areas and has shortcomings in other areas; together, we are complete. Asking for help is a practice in humbleness.

You attend school to get an education to help you get a career. However, in your personal life you may face lots of challenges that slow you down and for which formal education didn't prepare you. We are talking about the type of challenges you may face in your day-to-day interactions with people. If you have a problem in any part of your life, it is most likely because you have not educated yourself enough in that area of your life. If you feel stuck and do not have the life that you want, think about where you are stuck and in which phases of your life you haven't received the education that you need. For example, you might be very successful in your career, but have a relationship problem, because you neglected to improve your interpersonal skills. However, if allowed to continue, such personal relationship difficulties can affect your career as well.

With self-improvement, you will explore and nourish your abilities to be able to find the areas of your life that need improvement. In that way, you are making your liabilities your assets. Acknowledging your shortcomings, working on them, pushing your limitations, and asking for professional help are the most effective ways to improve and expand your aptitudes. Self-improvement requires flexibility and open-mindedness. When you decide to develop new skills, you acquire abilities that expand and nurture your life. Learn who you are as a person and where you are in your life to have an understanding of where you want to go. When you understand yourself, you have the ticket to understanding others.

In the process of self-improvement, you usually need guidance to help you become more than who you were. Self-improvement facilitates productivity, which means that you can use your abilities to create something greater than yourself. As mentioned earlier, a tree must grow for a long time before it is able to bear fruit. Ask for help from others to improve yourself mentally, emotionally, and physically. When you learn to listen to others, then you earn the right to be listened to; learn to understand yourself and then you earn the right to be understood.

To embark on self-improvement requires the power of vulnerability: you need others and others need you. The simple fact of knowing that you are not alone can help dissipate feelings of fear.

There are always two components in the learning structure: a child and a parent, a student and a teacher, an athlete and a coach, an apprentice and a journeyman, or a mentee and a mentor. There is no Olympic champion without a professional coach. Even ancient stories about learning start with two people. As Audrey Hepburn said,

> *"You have two hands: one hand is to help yourself, the other hand is to give and receive help."*

You will learn and grow faster with the help of an expert who has a deeper understanding of the solution. You need someone who is professional and outside of yourself to look at you from your inside out. A qualified person is able to guide you in a way that compresses years of education into a one-hour session of wisdom and solution. The literal meaning of "time is money" is that we sometimes waste our resources when we try to figure everything out on our own. For example, we go to the doctor with a sore throat to find out whether we have a simple viral infection or a serious bacterial infection that requires antibiotics.

Life becomes meaningful when you have a deeper understanding of yourself. If you want to stay strong, you must ask for professional help to continue your growth and become more powerful.

When you read books, you will acquire general knowledge about yourself and the world around you. However, you cannot gain knowledge from books that you haven't read. No matter how much you educate yourself, there is nothing that can take the place of the self-awareness that you can gain from a professional life coach. A counsellor will help you advance your understanding by obtaining clarity about your inner-self and the situation at hand. The real power lies in clarity. Clarity gives you the vision to control the wheel and steer it towards the change that you want. With clarity, you will understand the application of the power to change. You are powerful and capable, but your real capability will manifest itself in how you respond to a situation.

Change is part of life, and change moves downstream, just as every living thing eventually fades and ends. For example, a flower fades to its natural death but we can keep the resulting seeds and plant them for new growth. The option here is to let the plant die or plant the seeds. In this way, your personal growth is also optional. You need to find which seeds you have to plant and which ones you must stop planting. You may need an expert to help you recognize which is which. It is only through conscious choice and being able to admit that we need help that we will achieve growth.

Up until only a couple of decades ago, if somebody could not read or write they would have been considered illiterate. Today, in the digital age of fast information and communication, if you do not get help to work on your emotional intelligence, you are emotionally illiterate. Both the cause and result of not asking for help are to continue to have low confidence.

There is an unspoken rule in the constitution of our lives that, in every transition, there is a hand to help us make changes in our personal growth. Life is an evolving process and the growth features an equation with two sides. When we come into this world, our parents are there to be our helpers and providers; we rely on them to help us stand on our own feet. When we go to primary school, we have a teacher to help us learn; when we go to middle or high school, we have more teachers; and when we go to university, we have the help of professors, supervisors, and committees. Personal relationships partner us with a person and we become part of the family of that person. Furthermore, we need the help of institutions to formalize our marriages. If you think you do not need professional help or help from others, you have not paid attention to the structure of life because it started with the help of at least one parent. As we grow up and become more of who we are, we need the help of more people; when we become adults, we need the help of a community.

Counselling is like the parent who holds your hand while you learn to stand on your own two feet in each phase of your life.

You seek professional help for your car, yet, when it comes to you own well-being, you might not be a priority on your own list. You think you can do it all on your own. For example, if the sole of your shoe has a hole in it, you can have your shoe repaired; but, the majority of the time we don't spend any money to improve our own souls. Only if you put yourself on your own priority list will your life get better. By changing your perception about your emotional well-being and emotional growth, you can improve your life. When you get better, everything in your life gets better with you. Professional help can be the second set of eyes needed to show you where you are on the map of your life, where you want to go, and what you need to do to get there. Sometimes we are like an old car: you can change all of the seats and refresh the paint, but if the engine is not running it is only a nice skeleton; the car will not function properly. Sometimes your engine needs to get updated and repaired, and if you are aware of this, you know that your engine needs a check-up and tune-up. *You need to have the self-confidence to acknowledge this need about yourself.*

For low-confidence people, counselling and therapy for emotional well-being may be seen as *taboo*. You earn the right to tell yourself that your needs matter, then you allow yourself to ask for help or seek professional development to reach your full potential. Confronting your shortcomings, pushing your limitations, and asking for the guidance of an expert are the most effective ways to improve and expand your abilities.

No one is meant to take the journey through hard times alone. There is power in surrounding yourself with people who will help and support you, even when you do not have a strong sense of who you are or what is happening around you. The beauty is that, by sharing your weaknesses, you facilitate your own growth in ways that you didn't predict.

"No man will make a great leader who wants to do it all himself or get all the credit for doing it."

Andrew Carnegie

You can choose to grow by working to improve yourself, or you can get stuck, stay stale, and not harness that power. You can choose to believe that you know it all but this will stifle your growth. Confident people ask for help and dare to be vulnerable, while insecure people deny their need for help, refuse to ask for help, and get trapped in the past. For confident people, all that matters is that they resolve problems and find solutions. Everything is about the opportunity to learn and develop their potential to the fullest. Confident people are ambitious and eager to succeed. They go against the wind like an airplane. Asking for help with humbleness comes from confidence. If you ask for help with shame, you see asking for help as a sign of inferiority and you might be asking with contempt in your request. If you ask for help with arrogance, you will be denied the support of others because people hear your words but feel your contemptuous attitude.

Remember, you can ask for help because you want to upgrade an average quality to a good quality or good skills to great skills. You might play soccer at an average level but, by asking for professional help, you can upgrade your abilities to a higher level. The same applies to life; you might be doing well, but by going to counselling you become great or go from great to greater.

You can move towards self-improvement or get stuck and lose power because you want to say you did it all by yourself. You can never steer your life in a good direction and reach extraordinary results if you are rigid and do not ask for help. The prize for not getting help is minimal. Doing everything by yourself only results in a flag that says "all the credit is mine" or "I did it all by myself". And the prize of "I did it all by myself' is loneliness, while the prize of asking for professional help is building confidence.

Now let's discuss the last, but not least, habit of building a greater you.

Chapter Twelve: Making Decisions

"My only fixed truth is a belief in people: A conviction that if people have the opportunity to act freely and the power to control their own destinies, they'll generally reach the right decisions."

Saul Alinsky

Decide! In many instances, improving confidence requires that you have the courage to make a decision. At times, it is far better to make a poor decision than not to make one at all. When you make a poor decision, you can adjust your decision in the process and you are not stuck; but if you make no decision, you are stalled and there is no chance for correction. Successes come from poor decisions more often than from not making any decision at all. The poor decision you make becomes a learning experience, and subsequent decisions become more sound decisions. Success comes from making decisions, and in the process of life the poor decisions are the seeds of good decisions.

A fulfilled life is a life filled with decisions; confident people make decisions. Because confident individuals are aware that opportunities are limited, they will be prepared to make the decision to grab an opportunity the minute it is available. Making decisions is also very meaningful for the confident people; they take ownership of their decisions and hence are in charge of their own lives. The moment you make a decision, you can change your life for the better.

Why, you might ask? Because when you make a decision, you start to move, take action, and come out of being stuck. You can never be sure as to how something will play out — so let the plan for how it goes to be the job of the universe. Your job is to make the decision even when you don't know exactly how you will get there. Consider this analogy, you make a decision to visit a dear friend who lives far away and you have not seen him or her for a while. In this case, the details of transportation type or route you will take become secondary to your goal of reaching to your friend. The important thing is that you made the decision and that you will figure out the "how" as you proceed with your plan. Sometimes you have to take a detour due to road construction or change your direction or timing because of heavy traffic; this is just real life. The magic is that once you decided and started to take action, you are capable of sorting out the details.

Your decisions count! The combination of all your decisions, big or small throughout your life is what shapes how you are living. As Stephen Covey said,

"I am not a product of my circumstances. I am a product of my decisions.'

So, if you are not happy with one or more aspects of your life, it is usually not because of a single bad decision; rather it is likely because of repeating a number of bad decisions over and over or not making any decisions at all. A great deal of problems that you may have are there perhaps because you did not make a decision when you should have, or you did not take responsibility for your own decision, or worse, you followed someone else's decision about your own life. So, if you are not making a decision because you are worried about the details or worried about what if you made the wrong choice, rest assured that a single wrong decision about a trivial aspect of your daily life is unlikely to change your whole life. It becomes a problem only if you allow bad choices to become a way of living or become a routine negative habit, which will begin to bring the flow of negative consequences into your life.

Confident people fully participate in their own life by making their own choices, while being aware of the consequences of their meaningful decisions. This includes going with the best option at the time, given the information they had about the existing circumstances. This is how life works in general. When you make a decision and stand by it, it means you are using your own personal power. In other words, your power resides in your ability for decision-making. The moment you make a decision, you unleash your power within. This is because you recognized that you have the power to decide and chose to exercise that power by taking the action you deemed appropriate at the moment.

When you make a decision, you are putting yourself on the "cause" side and not the "effect" side of your life. People with low confidence usually do not see the importance of making decisions or perhaps decision-making is not an important part of their lives.

Think of an opportunity to make a decision as being given a ballot to vote. In a democratic society, people have the power to select their government officials on certain single days — election days — when there is an opportunity to participate, make a decision, and cast a vote. If you vote, you are exercising your power over government. If you indeed vote and think you chose based on your principles and the information you had, you can rest assured that no matter the result you can live more peacefully even if your candidate didn't win or didn't turn out to be who you though would be. Those who avoid making decisions, either avoid voting all together or it would take them such a long time to decide that the voting opportunity may pass. Therefore, in either case, such individuals would have to live by the choice of others.

Delaying decision-making to a later time or taking too long to decide, is often a sign that the decision-making process has become an emotional process; overcoming these emotional hurdles is often difficult. Therefore, the first solution for anyone who has difficulty making a choice is to start gaining control over their emotions.

Some individuals must be pushed against a deadline to make a decision, due to their anxiety over the potential consequences of making a mistake. For instance, when they are asked to do their taxes, they wait for the deadline to arrive when there is literally no further time to delay. They may do so because they are afraid of making mistakes or afraid of not making the perfect decisions. They may take a long time to come up with the perfect plan and therefore may lose the momentum to do it on time, and sometimes they even miss the deadline and would have to pay a penalty for being late. When you are too busy coming up with the perfect plan, you are worried about making a mistake and so you will find yourself being stuck or trapped. As Napoleon Hill said,

"The man of decision cannot be stopped! The man of indecision cannot be started! Take your own choice."

If you know what you want, and more importantly, know *why* you want it, you will figure out the "how". In other words, when your "why" is big enough, the planning will work itself out in time. If you only focus on the "how" of your decision, it becomes an emotional task, and you get stuck in whether or not your decision is perfect. This creates anxiety and the anxiety takes your focus away from the decision itself and puts it on the process instead. You might be afraid of the risks and want to take no risks at all. Therefore, you may actually make the biggest mistake by wasting time just trying to figure out the "how".

For some, to make a decision in any given situation, the pressure and stress must be very high to get them over the fear of making a mistake. They avoid making decisions as much as they can and literally rely on others to make even the simplest daily decisions for them. In other words, they make a decision only when they are either obligated to or when they reach a dilemma, a conflict, or a fork in the road. However, what they may not consider is that, if they don't make a decision when they need to, they may lose the momentum altogether and that's an even bigger mistake. Those who overanalyze every decision, will frequently miss the opportunity. They need to know there is no such thing as a perfect decision. However, not making decisions can make you inexperienced and that introduces pain in your life. Every situation that calls for a decision is a step forward on the path of progress towards the life that you want. *When you make decisions, you build confidence.*

Some may even get stuck because they are afraid to take action altogether, and even the biggest fear does not compel them to make a decision. These individuals are followers and live with the decisions and choices that others make for them, as if they live a life by default and conformity. In other words, they do not show up in their own life, because they are afraid that they may not be good enough to make decisions on their own or do not have the courage to stand up for their own decisions. Those who simply follow other people's choices miss the opportunity to practice their power in a meaningful way. As a result, they must deal with the consequences of the choices of others and therefore are constantly unhappy, and feel miserable and victimized. If they choose not to participate in decision-making, there may come a point when they cannot make any meaningful decision. They will then be forced to live as followers and make submissive decisions with little or no awareness or thought. That is why those who don't make their own decisions, are at the effect side of their own lives, not the cause side.

There is another group of people who don't have the confidence to make decisions for themselves, but can easily make decisions for others. They don't know what to do with their own lives and are therefore totally blind towards their own reality. Those who decide to take care of other people's lives will, in reality, take care of no one. In case of an emergency while on an airplane, you are supposed to put the oxygen mask on yourself first so you are able to take care of someone else. This is because you will be unable to take any action to save someone else if you suffocate first. *What you cannot give to yourself, you cannot give to anyone.* Therefore, people who are busy making decisions for others, instead of themselves, tend to blame others for their own lives and get stuck in frustration and anger. They feel the burden of others because they have voluntarily put that load on themselves. You must know that if you blame others, you see yourself as a victim of others and not the hero of your own life. Consequently, you lose confidence in yourself. You might feel like a victim of others because you did not make a victorious decision and handed your ballot over easily to someone else. Furthermore, you might make a decision based on following others and then blame them when things don't work out as expected. If you blame others because you are not making your own decisions, then you have sentenced yourself to live in an unhappy state.

To make good decisions, you have to learn to control your emotions and stay focused on your own life. You might make poor and impulsive decisions when your emotional power has not been properly harnessed or managed. By this, I mean you have to master your emotions, and control them from becoming too excessive (be it too positive or too negative) when you need to make a decision. Therefore, you should not make an important decision when you are too emotional. When you are too angry, too happy, too sad, too busy, and even too peaceful, you are more likely to make a poor decision. For example, when you are too peaceful, you are likely to choose to follow any decision, even a poor one. When you are too happy, you may be oblivious to see the whole picture, and when you are too angry, you may make the most regrettable decisions of all. When you are too sad, you might make decisions that become the biggest loss of your life. When you are too excited, you may make the most impulsive decisions of your life. To make a sound decision, you need the strength and power that comes from mastering your own emotions.

To respond shows confidence, while to react shows lack of confidence. To properly respond requires you to pause, think, gain control over your emotions, and only then make a decision. When you react, you are letting the urge for immediate retaliation take over your decision-making process and your emotions will get the best of you.

Each of us must confront our emotional turmoil and sort out our feelings. The decisions that accumulate throughout your life determine your destiny. Every time you make a decision, you have the option to make adjustments to the direction of your life. In that way, you begin to move towards that destiny. Your life is a direct result of all of your decisions. Those who do not make decisions are like pedestrians who stand in the middle of the road; they may get run over by life's oncoming traffic. So, if you want to have a fulfilled life, you have to have a life with many decisions. You build confidence by making decisions and owning them. Owning your decisions means that you take responsibility for the results of your own decisions.

It is the owning of the consequences of your decisions that makes you a real adult. Your life stays still and problems stay unresolved if you do not make decisions. Wherever you see progress in your life, a decision must have been made. Decisions are the starters of your engine and they make things move and happen. It is not the circumstances that create your life's situation, it is your decisions.

It is your responsibility and no one else's to make decisions for yourself, and you will feel stronger by making decisions rather than leaving them to someone else and then blaming the consequences on that person. If you live by this advice, you have the power to change your life.

Therefore, you make a decision when you start to take action. You make decisions when your desire for wanting is greater than your fears. Sometimes you make the right decision, and sometimes you correct the previous decision to make things right. In the end, making a decision fulfills your greatest potential.

It is your ability to control your emotions that help you make better decisions. Sometimes one decision makes a huge change in your life because that decision is made out of many other small decisions, and it becomes the last piece that tips the cascade of dominos. All that matters is living consciously and using your ballot to vote wisely to make the change when you have the power to do so. A sound decision comes from practice by making many decisions. A fulfilled life is a life in which you harness your emotions before you make a decision.

> *"Successful people are decisive people. When opportunities come their way, they evaluate them carefully, make a decision, and take appropriate action. They know that indecision wastes time that could be spent on more productive tasks."*
>
> Napoleon Hill

CONCLUDING REMARKS FOR SECTION 3

In the preceding section, we introduced 12 habits of mind that can help you build high confidence. In my experience, these are the most important positive ways of thinking that can transition your life towards total self-confidence. To believe in yourself and your unique inner talents and to define yourself as clearly as you can are two of the most fundamental and essential aspects of building self-confidence. Major next steps include working towards your personal growth by taking responsibility for your actions, dealing with challenges of life head-on, be open-minded and learning from anyone and from any situation, and making decisions on time and with a cool head in order to accept upcoming opportunities in your life. Towards the goal of building your high confidence, you also need to be process-oriented and value effort as much as the prize, while being goal-oriented and develop the discipline to stay focused, keep track of your achievements to remind yourself of your self-worth at rough times, have a positive anticipation and outlook towards life, think, and behave like a leader by showing consideration and courage to make different choices, and continuous movement on the path of self-improvement.

While most people can identify a need to work on most of these habits, some may find particular habits to be more relevant to their circumstances. As discussed in Section 2, once you identify certain negative habits of mind you must replace them with these positive habits rather than leaving a void. You may also recognize certain positive habits that are already part of your strong character. Use them to your advantage and to incorporate other habits to complement your power tool box in building your high confidence.

In the next section, we will discuss some of the effects of self-confidence on personal wealth and well-being.

EFFECT OF CONFIDENCE ON HEALTH AND WEALTH

Chapter One: What Self-Confidence Can Do for You

Confidence helps you deal with the challenges of life. If you are confident, you believe in your abilities and feel hopeful that you can do things that come your way. You are also more willing to try new things, and this helps you learn.

As a therapist, I have realized that confidence is one of the most important elements in health and happiness. Confidence is an essential part of building a stronger, healthier, and happier version of you.

The best way to help and empower yourself is to have enough self-confidence to obtain what you want for yourself. With the realization of your own potential and self-confidence in your ability, you can also make better decisions.

It is essential to do what you believe is right, even if others mock or criticize you for it. You must be willing to take risks and go the extra mile to achieve better things in life. When you are waiting for others to congratulate you on your accomplishments, you are diminishing your self-confidence.

Confident thinking is to accept compliments graciously while at the same time admitting your mistakes and learning from them. Confident people are positive and believe in themselves and their abilities. They also believe in living life to the fullest. Low self-confidence can be self-destructive and often manifests itself as negativity. As it has been said,

"We aren't what we think we are, but what we think - *we are!"*

Anonymous

After briefly talking about what confidence can do for us, let's look at the relationship between confidence and health.

Chapter Two: Self-Confidence and Health

People who lack confidence are afraid of the gap between themselves and their dreams. To reach your dreams, you must pass through the tunnel of your fears. Lack of confidence comes from a lack of discipline, and lack of discipline comes from a lack of solid character. You build character by being consistent. The two biggest fears of human beings are either *"I am not good enough"* or *"I am not loveable"*. Your internal evaluation system comes from your level of confidence. If you feel you are good enough, you will act accordingly. Conversely, you might not think highly of yourself because you think you are not good enough. You will have better health and well-being if you think highly of yourself because you evaluate everything from the lens of possibilities; however, if your level of confidence is low, then you see everything as a defect, and then these defects become your normal. You can even heal yourself from an illness or a serious disease if you think positively and evaluate yourself positively. The result of this positive thinking about yourself causes you to see yourself as bigger than the problem, or see the problem as smaller than you. It sometimes can be helpful to think of the problem at hand as a hockey puck. That way, you can view the problem much smaller than yourself and can easily envision hitting it as far away as you can.

Not seeing yourself as good enough affects your evaluation system, which in turn affects your decision-making. No one can define your evaluation system and you cannot adopt it from someone else either. If you are not confident when you think about yourself and your abilities, examine how you routinely evaluate yourself.

To be able to overcome low confidence you need to have an open mind about it and examine your life patterns, especially what and how you are thinking about yourself. You need to get rid of what is not helping or working, and replace them with new habits that will help you become more confident.

Some say the difference between an incredible dish and a mediocre one is the confidence, faith, and pride of the chef in their abilities. They believe when you eat a mediocre meal, perhaps you are tasting the doubt of the chef, and that the food has the flavor of the energy that went into it while being cooked. This same analogy can be applied to people. When you like the energy of a person, it probably stems from their positive sense of self or their 'flavor'. On the other hand, some people have a sense of doubt, which manifests as a lack of confidence or lack of trust in themselves. When you have self-confidence, you realize that not doing what others are doing does not mean you are failing or falling behind. You are charting your own course and staying true to yourself, even though it would be easier to join the crowd. You are creating a life you can fall in love with, instead of falling in line. You are finding the courage to do what's right for you, even though it might be uncertain, scary, or hard. Give yourself some credit, because these are all reasons to be proud of.

No matter how happy someone might seem, they too have moments when they question if they can go on. No matter how confident someone may look, there are times when they feel unsure and insecure. No matter how strong someone may appear, they too have days when they feel like they are falling apart. Being a human means you have a combination of messy and prideful days; you are not alone and not the only one who has pain in your life from time to time. So, define yourself as worthy and capable, think positive about yourself and give your best in whatever you do and you will be amazed how your confidence will grow. A confident mind will improve your physical and mental health.

Thus far, we mostly talked about how to build self-confidence, so in the next chapter, let's also briefly explore what happens if there is too much confidence.

Chapter Three: Is There Such a Thing as Too Much Confidence?

Too much of a good thing can be bad, and this applies to confidence as well. When people stop growing, they can become overly confident and lose their sense of humbleness. This further eliminates the need to learn and grow, and can lead to showing signs of arrogance. As Thomas Dewer said,

> *"If you think you know it all, you are missing something".*

Just as having too little confidence can prevent you from taking risks and capturing opportunities (in school, at work, in your social life, and beyond), having too much confidence can make you come across as arrogant, and then you are more likely to stumble into unforeseen obstacles.

To be successful, you must have a high enough level of confidence, but not too high levels which can turn into a rigid sense of entitlement and expectancy that creates a fragile personality. The Titanic ship sank because those in charge had too much confidence in its abilities, thinking it was invincible. When you are too confident, you lose touch with reality and take things for granted. Overconfidence brings a halt to your success and becomes a judgment. It's easy to become overconfident when you are ignorant and do not have consideration for others. Overconfident individuals try to make others feel inferior to make themselves feel superior, but the price they pay is the resentment they attract. People who are overly confident also think they already know everything and do not see a need to learn.

Now that we talked about the need for a balanced level of confidence, next I would like to make a clear distinction between self- esteem and self-confidence, because many use these concepts interchangeably.

Chapter Four: Differences Between Self-confidence and Self-esteem

Self-esteem is the gift of inspiration that radiates within you. It is something that is difficult to pin down intellectually, yet is undeniably recognizable in how you feel about yourself. When you have self-esteem, you are calm and have access to your ultimate wisdom. You can sense all of your powers are aligned and have arisen within you. You notice a source within you, a sanctuary in which all of your power lies, that makes you feel calm, collected, strong, and worthwhile. In the core of your being is an inspiration that resonates deep within you and can lift you high enough to be the creator of the life that you want. Your recognition of self-worth and your high spiritual energy, which is your essence, is meant to embrace your whole life. When you feel this resonance, that is the moment that you comprehend your worth, which is reflected in a feeling of calmness and congruency. You don't need to prove yourself to anyone; it's as if you feel a soothing drizzle is flowing deep inside you. You feel you are worthy; you can enjoy your own company as well as the company of others and are content with the steps that you are taking. When you feel your own worth which stems from your own abilities, you have a desire to be creative and continue to create more with your skills.

Self-esteem is the sum of how you feel about yourself and your worth. While self-confidence is what you think about yourself and the trust you have in your abilities, self-esteem is the sense of validity you have with yourself. When you have the courage and faith that you can do something, you have self-confidence but when you know that the worth of your effort comes from within, you have self-esteem. Self-confidence and self-esteem can become interconnected since how you feel about yourself reflects onto how you value your achievements and the worth of your achievements.

What you think about your abilities comes from your self-confidence, how you feel about your performance stems from your self-esteem. When you think 'you can', you are 'confident', but when you fall along the way, you need self-esteem to pick yourself up, feel good, energized, and poised to reach the destination. Self-esteem is not dependent on the level of your success, love, or the approval of others, all of which are separate from you. Esteem comes from your inner source of joy, courage, and curiosity. If you want others to make you feel good about yourself, you lack self-esteem. When you want others to appreciate you and your work, it is because you do not know your worth. When someone is looking for the approval of others, they see themselves as an object for auction, where others put a price on them. In other words, their value is at the mercy of others. Having low self-esteem takes the joy and happiness out of life. When you have low self-esteem, you will have low energy, and this will drain your contentment and hinder your progress in moving forward.

In the next chapter, let's review all the concepts we discussed thus far.

LAST WORDS

Throughout this book, we first discussed the importance of identifying and breaking the negative habits of mind that rob you of confidence. We then put even more emphasis on building and empowering positive habits of mind to nourish your confidence. We intentionally did not dwell on what might have happened in your past or who might have damaged your confidence; instead we focused on how to build your confidence on your own; the idea being to help you move from the effect side to the cause side of your life.

Remember that you must first define yourself and really know who you are as clearly as you can before you can observe growth and expansion in your life.

A key to success is learning how unique you are, being true to your own authentic self, and knowing your main goals in life. Study your purposes carefully and be interested in learning about them, but also be ready to challenge your unproven values just as you must be ready for all other challenges on your way. Without challenges, there is no growth.

People, businesses, communities, and countries are different because of how they allocate their money and resources. One of the most important investments for anyone should be to invest in own training and learning and in expanding own knowledge, skills, and understanding. You must know that if you stop growing, you will fade with depression and regression. To feel fulfilled, you must have a burning desire for learning, and then you will have a zest for life. You must rejuvenate yourself by giving yourself the gift of learning new skills. Remember, "LEARN to be able to EARN"; the more understanding and knowledge you acquire, the more wealth and wisdom you will attract.

Congruence between your *wants* and *needs* makes your life more productive and effective. Apply what we discussed in this book to become a confident person and make your potential work for you, instead of against you. When you find your gifts and talents, you have found your wealth, peace, and confident.

If you follow the system described in the preceding chapters, you can put in place your actions so that all the questions related to why, what, and how are aligned towards solutions, and the process becomes fluid and productive. Problems appear when there is no correct system in place; apply the correct system and there will be no room for problems. When you achieve your high confidence, you will know that the correct system is in place.

To be able to blow your own horn, to have a great life, and to find new avenues to express your creativity, you must have clarity of who you are, who you want to be, where you are, and where you want to be. You have to know where you are on the map of your life.

Invest in learning by reading books and getting professionals to help you broaden your horizons of understanding. I am a therapist, life coach and mentor but I too use the professional help of my mentors and colleagues from time to time and have seen the miraculous results of learning from them. A competent professional can compress a decade of self-learning into a one-hour session, and can show you the steps you need to take in your journey. View this book as a map, and my words as the tour guide to your destination. The investment you make towards advancing yourself is the magic that makes you more capable of trusting yourself to do more, be more, and have more.

"The most important relationship you can all have is the one you have with yourself, the most important journey you can take is one of self-discovery. To know yourself, you must spend time with yourself, you must not be afraid to be alone. Knowing yourself is the beginning of all wisdom."

Aristotle

To ask for help requires the power of vulnerability: you need others and others need you. Because you learn and grow with others, you can claim all you want, but the truth shows up when you are with others. Doing things with others will make you better and can increase the value and motivation for you to do your best. The nature of companionship will satisfy your desire and can help you leap towards your vision. If you want to stay strong, then ask for help to continue to be powerful and get more powerful. When you humbly ask for help, you must know your wish is worthwhile. To add value to your life, you must know that you have value. When you ask for help, take yourself as seriously as you take the demands of your loved ones when you help them. You earn the right from yourself that your wish matters, which then allows you to ask for help or seek professional assistance. Confronting your shortcomings, pushing your personal limitations, and asking for professional help are the most effective ways to improve and expand your abilities. All the rights are earned when you give them to others first; when you listen to others and when you understand others, you earn the right to be heard and to be understood.

You can ask for help or be a person who knows it all, gets stuck, and is unable to grow. Confident people ask for help and have the courage to be vulnerable; insecure people deny their need for help and dig in their heels. For confident people, all that matters is that they resolve the problem and find the solution; everything is about the opportunity to learn and develop their potential.

Develop a discipline to do the things you need to do, when you need to do them, even if they are hard to do, until this discipline becomes part of you. Consistently practicing this discipline then will make doing things less difficult over time because it becomes part of your character and as a result you build self-confidence. After all, you can pretend to have certain characters and impress people temporarily, but once you develop a discipline into your character it becomes a supreme and real investment. People trust a person's nature before they trust that person's vision. People will look up to you as long as you continue to grow, because they see you have enhanced value to yourself and your life, meaning that you can add value to them.

When you build a consistent need to grow, one of the first things that you will develop is confidence. When growth is the essence of your inner being and your prime goal in life, then it will radiate as confidence on the outside. While good breeding in animals is inherent, people acquire their best characters as a result of intentional growth. A well-formed character is the result of practicing courage, determination, and persistence.

A well-formed confident character is one that has gained the trust of others by being productive and reliable. As a result, people have positive anticipation for you, and this becomes the positive energy that surrounds you and people will follow you and view you as a leader.

Life is a process of change: births to the new and deaths of the old. This life process has a purpose — growth — but ironically mental, emotional, personal, and spiritual growth are optional. You can choose to grow and if you do, you can figure out how to tap into your inner power, which will manifest itself as self-confidence.

http://www.caravancounselling.com

Printed in the United States
By Bookmasters